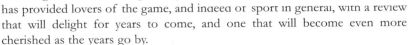

Legends of the Ash

'There can be few people more in love with his sport than Fullam. Like its predecessors *Legends of the Ash* is one to marvel at. Wonderful.'

The Sunday Times

'Invaluable for sentimentalists, journalists, enthusiasts, purists, revisionists.'

The Irish Times

'... another lovingly crafted hurling tome.... No self respecting hurling fan should be without one.

Sunday Tribune

The Wolfhound Guide to Hurling

'... to be treasured and handed down from generation to generation....'

The Irish Times

Off the Field and On

'There is so much history to mine in GAA history that even throwaway lines in this book will raise eyebrows.... For those with an avid love for our national games, it's a fine read....'

The Examiner

'The minutiae will fascinate GAA fans and the book is well endorsed by officialdom....'

Mayo News

'... a tribute to the human endeavour that has turned Gaelic Games into sports with international appeal.... Another must for GAA fans....'

Gaelic Sport

THE FINAL WHISTLE

BRENDAN FULLAM

WOLFHOUND PRESS

Published in 2000 by
Wolfhound Press Ltd
68 Mountjoy Square
Dublin 1, Ireland
Tel: (353-1) 874 0354
Fax: (353-1) 872 0207

British Library Cataloguing in Publication Data
A catalogue record for this book is available from the British Library.

ISBN 0-86327-8264

10 9 8 7 6 5 4 3 2 1

Photograph of Lory Meagher, p. 124, reproduced courtesy of Dan Hogan
Photographs of: the 1999 Tipperary Camogie Team, p. 175; the 1998 Galway
All-Ireland Football Champion Team, p.185; and The Artane Boys Band, p. 190,
reproduced courtesy of Inpho Photography.

The author and publisher wish to acknowledge the following for permission to
reproduce copyright material:
Extracts from *The Irish Times*, pp 149, 150, 153, 154 © *The Irish Times*
Extracts from *Irish Independent*, pp150, 151 © *Irish Independent*
Extracts from *GAA 100 Years — Commentary by Micheál O'Hehir*, pp 68-9, 91
© Gill & Macmillan, 1984

The publishers have made every reasonable effort to contact the copyright holders
of photographs and texts reproduced in this book. If any involuntary infringement
of copyright has occurred, sincere apologies are offered and the owners of such
copyright are requested to contact the publishers.

Cover photographs: Courtesy of Inpho Photography
Cover Design: Azure Design
Typesetting and book design: Wolfhound Press
Printed and bound in Spain by GraphyCems

BRENDAN FULLAM is a native of Ardagh, County Limerick, and a retired bank manager, who served in that capacity in Killorglin, County Kerry, The Crescent in Wexford, and New Ross. In his younger years his banking career took him to Killorglin, Kilrush, Clifden, Ballyshannon, Wexford and Tralee, and in each of these towns he played on the local hurling team. Gaelic Games are his passion, and his vision in meeting and interviewing the legends of hurling resulted in three unique and invaluable records of the game and its players — *Giants of the Ash*, *Hurling Giants* and *Legends of the Ash*. He is also author of *The Wolfhound Guide to Hurling* and *Off the Field and On* which is the predecessor to this book.

Other books by Brendan Fullam:
Giants of the Ash
Hurling Giants
Legends of the Ash
The Wolfhound Guide to Hurling
Off the Field and On

Dedicated to all those who have contributed to promoting our national pastimes and helped make the Gaelic Athletic Association the great organisation it is — in particular the silent ones, those who unselfishly look after and train the youth, the mothers who wash the jerseys and togs and the club officials whose voluntary work is a priceless asset.

CONTENTS

FOREWORD

One of the great treats for followers of sport everywhere is the opportunity to reminisce. We like nothing better than to look back, to hear and learn about the great players and great occasions of yesteryear. It is a pastime within a pastime. As an organisation, we in the GAA are fortunate that the history of Gaelic Games is wonderfully rich. It reflects the growth of a nation as well as the growth of the Gaelic Athletic Association. Over the past two decades the library chronicling that history has expanded greatly and in the credits the name of Brendan Fullam features proudly and prominently.

His growing volume of work is almost a library in itself and his books have become collectors' items for everyone who follows Gaelic Games. He has been prolific in his productivity and it comes as no surprise that following the success of his last book *Off the Field and On*, Brendan is back from the printers again with a new publication, *The Final Whistle*.

In previous books, the author has brought to life the personalities and the deeds of great players. Without them, many of the stories might have been lost and generations of followers might never have been able to enjoy the stories and recognise the feats of great players of the past.

With the care and feel for which he has become known amongst GAA historians, Brendan Fullam has once again captured the romance, drama, colour and passion of Gaelic Games. He starts his latest publication with a chronicle of the 1887 GAA Convention and takes us on a roller-coaster tour of the growth and development of the Association into the twenty-first century.

It is a uniquely personal view and that makes the book even more special. 'I Nearly Saw Mick Mackey Play' is the quirky title of a chapter that pays homage to one of the legendary figures of hurling. Brendan did see Christy Ring play and pays homage to the great man.

An attraction of the book is that, like Brendan's other books, it is not a conventional history. He chooses his subjects and gives them a personal touch. He looks at the rôle of the provinces, dedicates chapters to camogie, the Artane Boys Band, and media coverage of Gaelic Games. There is a modern feel to this book also with the achievements of Offaly since the 1970s and the rise of Clare hurling in the 1990s receiving special attention. In short, this book is an action-packed review of Gaelic Games.

In the GAA we recognise how fortunate we are that authors like Brendan Fullam have given so much time and energy to producing volumes of work dedicated to the affairs of the GAA. Their contribution has been invaluable.

Brendan has called his book *The Final Whistle* but I hope that is not an omen. It is far too early for Brendan to blow the final whistle on his career as an author. This book is proof of that.

Táimíd go léir fíor buíoch duit, a Bhreandáin, agus tá súil agam go mbeidh rath ar an saothar seo.

Liam Ó Maolmhichíl
Ard Stiurthóir
Cumann Lúthchleas Gael

PREFACE

Brendan Fullam typifies the true GAA activist. His love of the games and his great admiration for the players are obvious as the book unfolds.

This excellent work was indeed a labour of love for Brendan as indeed the GAA has been a labour of love for thousands and thousands of people down through the years. It was this labour of love which was the key to the great success of the GAA. People played the games out of sheer love for those games. Club officials and team mentors put in long hours day after day and year after year because they loved the games. And these very same games gave so much meaning to the lives of generations of people as they flocked to Croke Park, Semple Stadium or, most of all, to the local parish field.

I still have vivid memories of an elderly man coming to me after Offaly won their first hurling All-Ireland title in 1981. 'I never thought I'd live to see the day', he said. And as he tried to continue the conversation, he broke into tears. That's what the GAA means to so many people — a sense of place, a sense of identity, a sense of meaning and a fierce sense of pride.

Brendan Fullam is a key player in the GAA world as he records these precious moments. And these precious moments range from his interesting account of the 'Skirmish' at the 1887 Convention in Thurles where the delegates 'fought like dogs', to his description of the emergence of Clare hurling.

This particular record will bring much joy, happiness and entertainment (and the odd tear) to so many people. And of course the ensuing debates will be endless and even more entertaining.

Diarmuid Healy

INTRODUCTION

In field games the sound of the final whistle — barring a draw — signifies elation for the victor and disappointment for the vanquished. And yet, on calm reflection, it has to be admitted that, in the long-term, real reward is to be found in participation.

This was well summed up by five hurling stalwarts — all of whom tasted both victory and defeat — in their contribution to my book, *Giants of the Ash* (Wolfhound Press, 1991), and by that football supremo, Mick O'Connell, in his contribution to Brian Carthy's *Football Captains* (Wolfhound Press, 1993).

By way of introduction to *The Final Whistle*, I have recalled these great players and their words, which capture the spirit of sportsmanship and that of our national games.

John Maher was a key figure in the Tipperary defence for a span of sixteen years that ended in 1945. He loved the game. He had this to say: '... advice to any player: play the game for the game's sake.'

Pa 'Fowler' McInerney, a native of Clare, who hurled with Dublin as well as his home county, summed it all up in one simple sentence: 'I played the game with hurlers of the best that the game has produced and enjoyed every hour of it.'

Damien Martin, outstanding Offaly goalkeeper for over 20 years, epitomised what sport and games are all about, when he responded as follows after the great All-Ireland victory of 1981: 'Padraig Horan turned to me and said, "Wasn't it all worthwhile?" and I replied, "It would have been all worthwhile even if we didn't win."

Mick O'Connell, who strove for perfection in every facet of Gaelic football and for whom winning games and titles was not everything, had this to say:

'Anytime I got a ball coming from a distance it was a challenge to oneself to field that and catch it inch-perfect ... that you judged the ball perfectly, got up and got it in full flight. That's the personal satisfaction that stands out in my mind.'

The win-at-all-costs philosophy appalled him: 'If winning is everything, then I can't understand why people will say that sport is good for you. You teach children to win and lose and take the ups and downs.'

John Joe Doyle, a Clare man known to hurling followers as 'Goggles', was a prince of cornerbacks in the decade ending 1938; he wrote as follows:

And when the Great Recorder marks
Your score against your name,
'Twill matter not who won or lost,
But how you played the game.

In similar vein, Pat Stakelum, brilliant Tipperary centre halfback of the fifties had this to say:

When the final whistle for me has blown
And I stand at last before God's judgement throne,
May the Great Referee when He calls my name
Say, you hurled like a man — you played the game.

The foregoing players saw amateur sport for what it really is — a recreation to be enjoyed and cherished. It brought fulfilment and reward to their leisure hours. It left them with memories for future years — memories that will be enhanced by nostalgia with the passage of time.

This book, *The Final Whistle*, which deals with interesting aspects of our Gaelic Games is the companion volume to *Off the Field and On*.

It is August 2000 and I have just received a lovely card from Fatima from Austin Flynn of Waterford who featured in my book *Hurling Giants* (Wolfhound Press, 1994). His messages reads:

> *I visited the shrine this morning at 6.00 a.m. to pray for all the hurling people I knew. To simplify things for Our Lady I asked that all mentioned in Brendan's books who are gone ahead might end up in the winning dressing room and for those of us who are on the fringe of the team, She might use her influence with the Selection Committee to squeeze us in to the same place — even if we are only subs.*

A Skirmish in Thurles

The GAA's Convention of 1887 was held on 9 November, at the Courthouse in Thurles; it transpired to be an historic event. The meeting attracted a large attendance and special trains were arranged to carry the delegates (who numbered more than 1,600) to the venue.

The occasion has since been remembered as turbulent and the turmoil that occurred at it was in stark contrast to the sedate session that had taken place three years earlier on Saturday, 1 November 1884, at Miss Hayes's Commercial Hotel in Thurles, on the occasion of the founding of the GAA.

More than two decades later, when reflecting on the events of the 1887 Convention in *The Story of the GAA*, T.F. O'Sullivan had this to say:

The 1887 Convention held in Thurles was the most historic in the annals of the Gaelic Athletic Association, and was marked by incidents of unparalleled excitement.

There were many circumstances which invested the proceedings with unusual interest. In the first place the Executive had aroused a good deal of hostility owing to its vigorous action in suspending clubs and individuals who had refused to obey its rulings. These suspended Gaels were naturally determined to overthrow the governing body at the very first opportunity that presented itself; and were supported by strong articles which appeared in The Freeman's Journal *and* The Celtic Times, *denouncing the administration of what was contemptuously described as the "Hoctor-O'Reilly Executive". Many people deplored the withdrawal of Maurice*

Davin from the Presidency of the Association, and blamed the Executive for his retirement. The expulsion of the Royal Irish Constabulary, though that body was then very unpopular with masses of people, was regarded by some weaklings as introducing the political element into what was claimed to be a purely athletic organisation: and the "non-politicians" — those who were too meanly shoneen to identify themselves with a purely national movement, and too cowardly to openly oppose it - did all in their power to bring about the overthrow of the Executive.

The fact that men like the late Mr P.N. Fitzgerald, Cork, who made no secret of their desire to wipe out "the British name and nation" in this country, were identified with the Association, gave the organisation a complexion which made many timorous people uneasy and aroused the hostility of a large number of clergymen. Then again, the refusal of the Executive to accept the arbitration of Dr. Croke and Michael Davitt or any compromise in the Freeman's Journal *Club dispute regarding the handicapping, exposed the governing body to a good deal of criticism.*

In addition the Gaels of Tipperary — then the strongest Gaelic county in Ireland — had grievances of their own against the Executive. They claimed that Templemore had been improperly declared champions of Tipperary and that the venue selected for the holding of their county convention (Nenagh) was unsuitable. Many teams had also grievances, real or imaginary, in regard to the county and inter-county contests and were anxious to get even with the Executive.

It may be stated that there never was a governing body against whom was arrayed so many influences, and, on the other hand, it must be admitted that no governing body ever had behind it more loyal and enthusiastic supporters. The strong Nationalist views of the Executive, their vigorous action in crushing insubordination, and their earnest, if somewhat injudicious, efforts to maintain discipline, appealed to thousands of Gaels in all parts of the country, and accounted for the fact that they were able to withstand the attacks of the most powerful critics and the most insidious foes.

Looking back now calmly on the work of the Executive, it must be admitted that the members of the governing body made some mistakes, but they were the mistakes of strong men with strong views, determined to make the Association what it is to-day — not only a powerful athletic body, but a great national organisation.

The trouble which characterised the Convention of 1887 was sparked-off when the question of the Chairmanship was raised. Thus began a most acrimonious and unbecoming meeting. The official events unfolded as follows:

- P.N. Fitzgerald of Cork was proposed as Chairman by Alderman Horgan and seconded by T.P. Hoctor
- as an amendment, Major Kelly was proposed by Rev. John Scanlan CC, Nenagh
- P.N. Fitzgerald pointed out that he could not receive Fr Scanlan's proposition, as an amendment, as Major Kelly was an expelled member of the association.

There then followed much shouting, verbal abuse, cheering and counter-cheering which generated much confusion overall.

The chaos continued and at one stage, following some heated exchanges, there was an advance on the bench led by the clergy and their supporters. The reporters present had to jump to safety as matters stopped just short of blows being struck — sticks were brandished, furniture was broken and it was feared matters might develop into a riot.

Eventually at 2.45 p.m. — exactly an hour and a quarter after the proposals had first been made — Fr Scanlan, and all of the clergy present, left the meeting accompanied by their supporting delegates. Their exit was made to the derisive cheers of those who remained.

The meeting then proceeded without them and concluded at 7.00 p.m. Meanwhile, Fr Scanlan and his supporters held a separate meeting.

The day after the convention Dr Croke wrote as follows to the *Freeman*, saying:

> *Though not quite unprepared for a troubled, if not a turbulent meeting, and for certain unpleasant revelations with which my ears have been rendered familiar for some time, I could not at all have believed that the elements of mischief were so painfully present in the organisation as they now appear to be, and that evidence of the fact would have been so soon and so unmistakably given. Nothing, therefore, remains for me but to disassociate myself, as I now publicly do, from that branch of the Gaelic Athletic Association which exercised such a sinister influence over yesterday's proceedings.*

The *Freeman's Journal* also denounced the action of P.N. Fitzgerald and his supporters at the convention, and stated, on 11 November:

We do not desire to say one word against the motives of those who think that the rights of Ireland cannot be obtained by constitutional agitation, and who hold themselves morally justified in resorting to other means. Mr Herbert Gladstone the other day declared that the circumstances of Ireland would justify a revolution. The Earl of Beaconsfield stated the same thing a generation ago. Theoretically we do not deny the truth of that assertion, but what we do say is this, that nothing practically justifies an attempted revolution which has no possible chance of success. What we do say is that the men — be they few or many or their motives noble or otherwise — who would encourage the young men of Ireland to enter into an Association for revolutionary purposes are, whether knowingly or the reverse it matters not, playing the game of the enemies of the country, playing the game of the present government, and adopting the only possible method of defeating the otherwise assured success of Home Rule. What we do say is that anything which would sow dissension between the priests and the people of Ireland must inevitably lead to disaster. There never yet has been a revolutionary movement in Ireland every detail of which was not known to the government. If there be anything of the kind now on foot we are perfectly certain that the government know all about it. We are perfectly certain that they could put their hands upon every man connected with it whenever they thought fit, and we are perfectly certain that if they do not do so, it is because it is not their time, and because they would rather let the mischief ripen in order to utilise it for the purpose of destroying the Home Rule movement.

Mr Bennett, the President at that time, wrote to the *Freeman* on 14 November stating that the GAA was non-political and that there was no hostility between it and the National League or the priesthood.

The *Freeman,* for weeks, was filled with letters from priests and others denouncing the convention and declaring that it had been packed (there was a conviction amongst some that the men of physical force had aspirations in the political field and were attempting to dominate and supplant those who would take a constitutional approach). There were hundreds of resolutions to the same effect sent to the papers by different branches of the GAA. In addition, Mr Davin was called on to resume the Presidency of the Association and there were also demands for a new convention to be held.

The outlook for the GAA looked bleak but happily an amicable solution finally emerged.

On 22 November 1887, Dr Croke held a conference, at his residence in Thurles, with Michael Davitt and Maurice Davin. His aim was to try and repair the damage that had been caused and to take steps towards reconstructing the Association. On the same day, P.N. Fitzgerald met Michael Davitt separately and this too helped pave the way towards reconciliation.

Matters were further smoothed at a meeting of the Executive at Limerick Junction on 23 November 1887.

Finally, on 4 January 1888 a convention was held in Thurles in order to reconstruct the Association on the basis of suggestions made by Archbishop Croke who resumed as patron. Maurice Davin resumed as President.

P. N. Fitzgerald

Dr Croke was a visionary who foresaw the benefits that would flow to the Irish people and nation from a strong, vibrant and united Gaelic Athletic Association. He was a tower of strength to the GAA in its infancy and his support was invaluable. His overall contribution was immense, for, among other things, he was a diplomat and a pragmatist.

Thus ended the split in the Gaelic Athletic Association; a disastrous schism had been averted.

The Unfinished Championships

Only once in the history of the GAA — despite political and social unrest, a war of independence, a civil war, and two world wars — did the hurling and football championships remain unfinished. That was in 1888, the second year of such competitions.

Eighteen counties had been affiliated for the competitions that year and, in both hurling and football, the following draws were made:

Munster

Limerick v Clare in Limerick
Tipperary v Cork in Buttevant
Waterford (granted a 'bye')

Leinster

Dublin v Kildare in Dublin
Wicklow v Wexford in Wexford
Kilkenny v Queen's County (Laois) in Maryborough (Portlaoise)
Louth v Meath in Dundalk

Connaught

Galway v Sligo
Mayo (granted a 'bye')

Ulster

Cavan v Monaghan in Dundalk

The Munster Championships

In hurling, Clare (O'Gonnelloes) got a walk-over from Limerick (South Liberties) and this put them through to the final.

In football, Limerick (Commercials) lost to Clare (Newmarket-on-Fergus) at Birdhill by 1:3 to 1:0. It was a most surprising result as Limerick were the reigning All-Ireland champions at the time. However, an objection followed. This was based on the premise that the Clare team had players on duty from outside the parish of Newmarket-on-Fergus. The objection was upheld and Limerick were awarded the match. They then advanced to the Munster final.

On Sunday, 27 May in Buttevant, Tipperary (Bohercrowe) beat Cork (Lees) in a low-scoring football game — it finished 2 points to 1 point. Cork objected to Tipperary's victory on the grounds that their team was illegal; however, this was over ruled and Tipperary progressed to the next round.

On the same day Tipperary (Clonoulty) faced Cork (Towers) in hurling. Tipperary were leading by 2:1 to nil when, as recorded by T.F. O'Sullivan in *The Story of the GAA*, '... the match abruptly terminated'.

This was followed by an objection from Cork. A replay was then sanctioned and fixed to be played in Cahirmee. Tipperary were not impressed by either the decision to grant a replay or the venue that had been chosen. The men of Clonoulty decided to stay at home and bade farewell to the hurling championship. Thus Cork were due to meet Clare in the Munster hurling final, but this game apparently never took place

Tipperary won their next football match which was against Waterford (Kilrossenty); the game was played in Clonmel and ended on the score: 0:3 to 0:1. That victory paved the way for a Munster final meeting with Limerick at Pallas. The game was fixed for a weekday but Limerick (Commercials) failed to turn up. The team consisted of shop assistants and it may well have been that they were unable to avail of the necessary time off work to go and play the match. The upshot of their failure to attend was that the men from Tipperary were awarded the match and the county celebrated its first Munster football senior crown.

The Leinster Championships

Dublin had a double victory over Kildare at Clonskeagh on 3 June. The extent of their superiority is reflected in the following scorelines:

Football

Dublin (Feagh McHughs) 1:6; Kildare (Clane) 0:1

Hurling

Dublin (Kickhams) 3:6; Kildare (Monasterevan) 0:2.

Kilkenny and Queen's County (Laois) met in both hurling and football at Maryborough (Portlaoise) on 10 June. The final whistles signalled a Kilkenny double on the scores:

Football

Kilkenny (Kilmacow) 1:3; Laois (Ballinakill) Nil

Hurling

Kilkenny (Mooncoin) 2:2; Laois (Rathdowney) 0:2.

The Louth (Dundalk Young Irelands) v Meath (Dowdstown) football game, originally fixed for Dundalk, was switched to Drogheda where Louth were victorious on the score:

Louth 2:4; Meath nil.

The football match between Wexford (Blue and Whites) and Wicklow (Annacurra), played in Wexford, turned out to be a rough and controversial affair. Before the game finished spectators invaded the pitch. Wexford lodged an objection, alleging that Annacurra had players from outside the club. A replay was ordered and fixed for Dublin on 9 August. This game lasted for an hour and a half with the result in doubt right up to the final whistle. Wexford were the ones to advance, however, on the score: 1:3 to 1:2.

In Clonskeagh on 2 September, there was a double bill that produced the following results in football:

Kilkenny (Kilmacow) 2:1; Louth (Dundalk Young Irelands) 0:3.

Wexford (Blue and Whites) 0:4; Dublin (Feagh McHughs) 0:3.

The Leinster football final took place in New Ross on 23 September between Kilkenny (Kilmacow) and Wexford (Blue and Whites). The Noresiders won by 1:4 to 0:2.

In the Leinster hurling final, Kilkenny (Mooncoin) defeated Dublin (Kickhams) by 0:7 to 0:3. Thus Kilkenny became the first county in Ireland to achieve a provincial senior double — a success that they were destined to repeat in both 1900 and 1911.

The Ulster Championships

Like the Louth v Meath football match, the Monaghan v Cavan football game had been originally scheduled to be played in Dundalk. However, the venue was switched to Drogheda where the result was 2 points apiece. In a subsequent replay, Monaghan (Inniskeen) beat Cavan by 3 points to 1 point to take the first-ever Ulster football title. They weren't to win it again until 1906.

There is no record of any game that was played in Connaught in 1888.

The aforementioned series of games advanced the championships of 1888 to the following positions:

Ulster
Monaghan became football champions.

Leinster
Decisive results emerged in both hurling and football — a Kilkenny double.

Munster
Matters weren't as clear-cut in the southwest: Tipperary took the football crown, but no result was produced in hurling as the final between Cork and Clare wasn't played.

Thus far and no further did the championships of 1888 progress. The reason given is the 'US Invasion' (see the following chapter) by hurlers and athletes. And yet, it hardly seems a complete and satisfactory answer. The athletes — 48 in all — set sail for America on

16 September 1888 and began their return journey on 31 October. There was plenty of time left to complete the championships. It is worth remembering that the finals of 1887, the first finals, didn't take place until April 1888. Many subsequent finals ran very late. For example, the 1902 finals didn't take place until September 1904. Could it be that in those far-off and distant days of the infant GAA the prospect of being crowned All-Ireland champions didn't have the same status and glitter that is now associated with it? As against that, surely 'the honour of the little village' would have rated highly with the players.

Perhaps it was finance that halted the championships of 1888. It must be borne in mind that the 'US Invasion' was a financial flop.

Whatever the reasons, it is hard to understand why those still in the running didn't press matters — especially Kilkenny who were poised to bring off a great double.

Perhaps it was simply a manifestation of one of the many growing pains of an infant organisation, with a fragile structure, that had yet to come of age. Teething problems expressed themselves in many shapes and forms during the 1888 championships — and indeed continued to do so for many years afterwards — walk-overs, objections, counter-objections, unfinished games, failure to turn up and pitch invasion all played their part.

However, all that was in the dim and distant past. Given the structures that exist nowadays, it would be impossible to visualise or conjure up a set of circumstances that would lead to the non-completion of the championships in hurling and football.

THE US INVASION — 1888

The Fenian Brotherhood movement was founded in New York by John O'Mahony and, consequently, was very strongly supported in the United States. O'Mahony had taken part in the abortive 1848 rising of the Young Irelanders following which he fled to Paris. Shortly afterwards he went to America where he established the Fenian Brotherhood in 1855.

At that time, Canada was part of the British Empire and, in 1866, the Fenians in the US decided that they would effect an invasion of that territory. A couple of thousand Fenians took part in the action. It was, however, quickly subdued by the combined efforts of the Canadian authorities and the British troops that were stationed there.

No wonder, therefore, when I first heard — many decades ago now — of the US Invasion of 1888, I understood it to be something similar to the 1866 affair. However, I quickly discovered that I was wrong. On this later occasion, 'the invasion' was a peaceful expedition — a trip to the United States by Irish hurlers and athletes to perform and play exhibition games at several locations there.

Mick Hickey, of Carrickbeg, travelled with the party — he would have been in his early twenties at the time. It may, therefore, come as a surprise to many to learn that I had a telephone conversation with his son — also Mick — in early July 1998. He was in very good spirits and his memory of the past was crystal clear: he could still recite the poetry he had learned off by heart in his school days. He told me that his father, 'was the first man to bring a hurley to Carrick-on-Suir — he walked to Mooncoin for it'.

Mick still had the hurley his father used in the US in 1888. Imagine, a hurley over 100 years old!. We agreed to meet and talk about old times and 'battles long ago'. However, the Great Recorder intervened and called Mick on the twenty-third of that month to '*Solas na bhFlaitheas*' — 'a bourn in Paradise, where all the hurlers go'. He was 87. '*I seilbh ghrámhar Dé go raibh tú a Mhichíl uasail*'.

Mick (junior), of course, was also a famous hurler in his day. (He featured in my book *Giants of the Ash*). He had captained Waterford, in 1938 when they won their first Munster senior hurling title. They failed in the All-Ireland final by 2 points against Dublin that year. He was recalled to the right half-back position for the 1948 All-Ireland final against the same opposition, when Waterford successfully avenged the result of 1938.

At a meeting of the Central Council, held at Limerick Junction on 6 July 1888, it was decided to go ahead with plans to send a team of athletes and hurlers to the US.

The project had the full support of Michael Davitt and Dr Croke and both men subscribed to its funding. The Irish in America were enthusiastic about the idea. There was also much support for the scheme at home and both clubs and individuals contributed financially to help ensure its success.

The driving force behind the campaign was Maurice Davin and it was expected that £1,000 would be required to cover the expenses. The 'Invasion' party was to number about fifty people in all.

The main object of the expedition was to promote international Gaelic Games competition. However, the organisers of the trip had further aims. They had hoped that the 'Invasion' would lead to the establishment of GAA branches in the US, as well as annual hurling and athletic contests between Ireland and America. In addition, they were optimistic that, arising from such developments, the coffers of the GAA would benefit to the extent of enabling it to pay off its existing debts. Hopefully, with any surplus income over that, the GAA would also be in a position to finance prizes for international contests between all Celtic races, which it was thought might take place in 1889.

There were also aspirations to revive the Ancient Tailteann Games — *Aonach Tailteann* — where it had been the custom for Irish Clans to gather and combine festivity, business, music, sport and trade in one enormous fair. All these ambitions fitted into the ideal of reviving as many aspects as possible of Irish traditions, customs and pastimes.

With regard to 'The Invasion Teams' T.F. O'Sullivan, in his *Story of the GAA*, wrote as follows:

> *The athletes selected were (those with an asterisk before their names being also members of the hurling teams):- J.S. Mitchell, Emly; Dr. J.C. Daly, Borrisokane; *Pat Davin, Solicitor, Carrick-on-Suir, (brother of Maurice Davin); Wm. Real, Pallasgreen, *P. O'Donnell, Carrick-on-Suir; D. Shanahan, Kilfinane; *J. McCarthy, Staker Wallace Hurling Club, Limerick; *M. Connery, do; *J. Connery, do; W. McCarthy, Macroom; P. Looney, do; T.J. O'Mahony, Rosscarbery; P. Keohan, Dungarvan; T. Barry, do; T.M. O'Connor, Ballyclough; W. Phibbs, Glenville; *D. Power, Shanballymore; *J. Mooney, Ballyhea.*
>
> *The names of Messrs. Daniel Fraher, Dungarvan and J.P. O'Sullivan, Killorglin, were also mentioned as members of the Athletic team, but they did not travel.*
>
> *The hurlers, in addition to those who were also athletes, were:-*
>
> *Tom O'Grady, Moycarkey; J. O'Brien, do; J. Stapleton, Thurles; T. Ryan, Clonoulty; and W. Prendergast, Clonmel (Secretary of the Association); P.P. Sutton, Metropolitans, Dublin; G. Burgess, Dunleary (Kingstown); J. Furlong, Davitts, Dublin; J. Hayes, Faughs, do; Frank Coughlan, Kickhams, do; Jas Royce, Oulart Hill, Wexford; P.J. Molahan, Monasterevan; P. Fox, Mooncoin; M. Curran, Castlecomer; J. Grace, Tullaroan; J. Dunne, Rahan, King's County; J. Nolan, Dunkerrin do; J. Cordial, Kinnelty [sic], do; P. Meleady, Birr; P. Ryan, Rathdowney, Queen's County; J. McEvoy, Knockaroo, do; D. Godfrey, Murroe; J. Coughlan, Buttevant; M. Hickey, Carrickbeg; J. Rourke, Kilbane, Clare; J. Fitzgibbon, O'Gonnolloes, do; P. Minnogue, Tullas, do; Mooney, Ballyhea, Cork.*
>
> *Altogether there were forty-eight hurlers and athletes.*
>
> *The hurlers were divided into two teams, one captained by Tom O'Grady, and the other by P.P. Sutton, who also acted as the Special Representative of* Sport *in conjunction with the 'Invasion'.*

Mr. John Cullinane, Bansha, (now M.P) left for America a few weeks in advance for the purpose of making arrangements for the athletic contests and hurling exhibitions.

Messrs. Maurice Davin, President, R.J. Frewen, Treasurer, W. Prendergast and J.J. Cullen, Secretaries of the Association, Rev. J. Concannon, Tullamore; Mr. Thomas Harrington, Johnstown, Kilkenny and Mr. Jos Whelan, President of the Freemans Journal *Club, accompanied the teams.*

The Irish team sailed for the United States on board the *Wisconsin*, on 16 September 1888. They were most enthusiastically welcomed when they arrived in New York following their voyage, which had taken them nine days.

The following is a description of the invading Gaels by the *New York Herald*:

It would prove a difficult task to bring together at short notice a more splendid assemblage of specimens of manhood than the half-hundred clear-complexioned and clean-limbed, stalwart, bright-eyed, muscular, strapping and fine-looking young fellows who were grouped on the deck of the Steamship 'Wisconsin' at noon yesterday. The crowd would have inspired an artist in quest of a model for 'a picture of health'. They were the representatives of Ireland's muscular christianity culled from every county of the Emerald Isle — literally the flower of Erin's manhood. Their attire was as characteristic as their appearance. Their 'reefers', cutaways, ulster and inverness capes were of the soft, warm, national frieze. Most of them wore knee-breeches, and all carried blackthorns or furze sticks, that would more than prove a match for the hickory or locust of 'one of the finest'. Mr. John Cullinane their advance representative, 'sported a small

Mick Hickey

blackthorn tree, which, to use his own words, was 'historical, as it worked through the Mitchelstown riot.'

A hurling match between O'Grady's and Sutton's teams is thus described in the *New York Herald*:

The great gathering (in New York) enjoyed the hurling hugely, and when the stalwart Irish lads marched out, with their hurleys on their shoulders and in military form, the spectators gave them a cheer. They formed in lines in the centre of the field, the ball was thrown up, and then the fun began. Such leaping, jumping, running, hitting, and tumbling had never been seen on those grounds. Hardly a man missed a "welt", and there was not a man on the field who was not ambidextrous. Once the ball was cornered among half a dozen of each side, and heads, legs and hurlers were in inextricable confusion. To the stranger it seemed dangerous play, but the men, from long practise, never hit a head.

Exhibitions were given in New York, Brooklyn, Yonkers, Boston, Providence, Philadelphia, Lawrence, and Lowell, Mass., and Trenton, Newark, and Paterson, New Jersey. The Canadian tour was abandoned owing to the weather.

The 'Invasion' programme included: wrestling, high jump, long jump, hammer-throwing, slinging the 56-pound weight, putting the 16-pound shot, 120-yard hurdles and races varying from 100 yards to 5 miles.

The 'Invasion' was an athletic success with hurling proving extremely popular. Unfortunately, it was a financial failure.

T.F. O'Sullivan gave the following reasons for the failure:

- *The States were in the throes of a Presidential election.*
- *The weather for the most part was very wet, and militated against large attendances at the exhibitions.*
- *The advertising was not as effective as it might have been.*
- *There was a war waging between the two athletic organisations of America — the National Amateur Athletic Association and the Athletic Union, both of which were anxious to exploit the 'Invaders'. The Gaels held their exhibitions under the auspices of the Manhattan Athletic Club, which was affiliated with the NAAA, with the result that the Athletic Union refused to allow their athletes compete at any of the meetings in which the Gaels participated.*

All these elements contributed to the failure of the 'Invasion' from the financial point of view, and Michael Davitt paid a sum of £450 in order to meet hotel and other expenses incurred by the teams.

About twenty of the athletes who travelled remained in the US. Those who returned sailed for Ireland from New York on the *City of Rome*, on 31 October 1888.

To the best of my knowledge, no in-depth study has ever been carried out on the details or effects of this adventurous expedition. If it is done some day, its findings will be most interesting and would hopefully address the following questions:

Was it premature?
Was it too ambitious?
Was it coloured by idealism rather than pragmatism?
Did it have a missionary dimension to it— a spreading of Celtic culture?

Personally, and with the benefit of hindsight, I would say that, the answer to the first of these questions is 'no'. I have in mind the Parnell split of 1891 which, of course, couldn't have been foreseen in 1888. After the split, things got so bad within the GAA for so long that there could have been no question of an American trip.

However, in my view, the answer to the other three of the above questions is 'yes'.

One unfortunate result of the American trip was that Maurice Davin, President, left the GAA in January 1889 — never to return to the council chambers. He had been unfairly taken to task over the state of the Association's finances after the US Invasion.

It is impossible even to begin to quantify or measure the extent of the loss to the GAA of a man of

Michael Davitt

the calibre of Maurice Davin. One is talking of an athlete of national and international renown; a man who was held in the highest regard and who was well-known for his integrity. His calm disposition and keen intellect were qualities that would have been invaluable to the Association in its formative years. The loss of Maurice Davin was immense.

My Early Memories of Christy Ring

The first I ever heard about Christy Ring was from hurling enthusiasts in my native parish of Ardagh, in West Limerick, when they would recall the events of an epic contest that had been held in Thurles in 1944. The match was the Munster final — the bicycle final — Cork and Limerick locked in mighty combat in a replay that would decide who were the kingpins of Munster hurling.

The local commentators would talk about the final moments of what had been a hectic encounter — shaking their heads, exhaling and pondering the might-have-beens. It was a game where Limerick had held the lead from the third to the fifty-seventh minute and our experts would endlessly reflect on the likelihood that a possible All-Ireland crown had been snatched from Limerick's grasp in as sensational a finish as was ever witnessed on a hurling field.

A five-point Limerick lead had been cut to one point as time-added-on was being played. Then Johnny Quirke, veteran of 100 battles and one of hurling's greats, drew on all his experience to send the equaliser over for Cork. It looked like it was to be another draw.

Then suddenly, it all happened as Ring scored a sensational goal that still lives on in hurling lore. He gathered the ball around midfield and sprinted up the wing on a solo to within about ten yards of the end line. He then let fly an angled shot that produced a goal that was worth a king's ransom — one of the most timely of his long and illustrious career.

A later image of the man was captured for me through the eyes and voice of the late Micheál O'Hehir during the All-Ireland final of 1946 — the first hurling final I listened to on radio. It was coming close to half-time and Kilkenny were ahead of Cork by 5 points to 3. Within a minute of the half-hour whistle Gerry O'Riordan put Cork into the lead with a goal. Seconds later, Ring was away on a solo run from midfield as the Kilkenny backs retreated to cover the Cork men. I can still hear the voice of Micheál O'Hehir as he captured the excitement of each ten-yard piece of this solo run which split open the Kilkenny defence and left Jim Donegan alone in the Kilkenny goal with no chance.

It was a killer goal and a timely one that sent Cork to the dressing room at the interval with a 4-point lead and a big psychological advantage. They finished the hour by capturing their sixteenth All-Ireland title with the illusive Ring the star of the afternoon.

I first saw Christy Ring in the red jersey of Cork as I watched from behind the Canal Goal in the All-Ireland final of 1952 against Dublin — my first time attending a hurling final. Christy was in search of his sixth All-Ireland medal on that occasion. Time has dimmed my recollections of the details of the encounter, but in my mind's eye I can still see the personal duels of the first half between Christy at left half-forward and Des Ferguson who gave a fine performance in coping with the maestro. And every time the ball came their way there was a hum of expectation from the crowd for the spectators knew that at any moment in the hour Ring was capable of pulling off the unexpected, of giving his man the slip, of creating something out of nothing. Little wonder then, that every ball won and cleared by Des Ferguson was cheered by Dublin followers and neutrals alike.

A close, exciting first half was followed by a second half where the experience and class of Paddy Barry's men, coupled with the brilliance of Dave Creedon in goal, saw Cork gradually pull away for a comfortable 2:14-to-0:7 win. I remember also the superb goalkeeping of Kevin Matthews in the Dublin goal.

I saw Christy in other games too but, without a doubt, the most memorable of them all — that I saw — was the Munster final of 1954, at Limerick, where Cork faced Tipperary. It was their fifth successive

meeting in a Munster final: Tipperary had won in 1950 and 1951 and
Cork had emerged supreme in 1952 and 1953. By 1954, the rivalry had
grown intense — bordering, at times perhaps, on the unhealthy.

At the time of the 1954 final, I was stationed with the National
Bank in Killorglin (home of the great athlete and footballer J.P.
O'Sullivan who captained the famous Laune Rangers football team
back at the turn of the twentieth century). Transport to the game was
provided by John Murphy, Assistant Manager in the Provincial Bank.
John, a Corkman and avid supporter of its hurling teams, regularly
walked the beach at Rossbeigh — army style. He moved at speed and
was as fit as the proverbial fiddle.

On the 75-mile journey to the game we passed through Firies,
Farranfore, Castleisland, Abbeyfeale, Newcastle West, Rathkeale, Adare
and Patrickswell. Interspersed with general conversation and
recollections of hurling battles long ago, John, with pride in his voice
entertained Mick Lane and myself with memories of Cork teams and
in particular Christy Ring. He knew all about Christy —

> ... *won an All-Ireland minor medal as a sub in 1937 and as a half-back the
> following year; first played with Cork seniors in 1939, but he was very light then
> — only a slip of a fellow weighing about nine-and-a-half stone; he got a right
> baptism of fire to Munster championship hurling in the drawn-and-replayed final
> of 1940 against Limerick; he was marking Peter Cregan; he joined the Glen in
> 1941 — I think he made them. Did ye ever hear about one of his first games with
> Cork? He was a sub — 'twas a league game and coming towards the end Sean Óg
> said to him, 'Do you want to go in for a puck?' — 'Yes sir', said Ring. Now isn't
> that a good one?*

Soon we were in Limerick. *Giorruigheann beirt bothar.* We parked on
the Quay. John now set a hectic pace. It was left-right, left-right all
those miles to the Gaelic grounds. My youthfulness coped admirably
with the precision of his practised stride and swinging arms. This was
missionary stuff. An American once said — enthralled by a hurling epic
— it's a game for the Gods. We were on our way to worship with tens
of thousands of others as thirty men — great men all — battled for
glory.

John died a thousand deaths during the game. Only fleeting moments remain in my mind: the swaying crowd on the embankment, the tension that we sensed around us, the hawkers burrowing their way through a record crowd of 52,449 people with their baskets of fruit and ice-cream and chocolate bars, the duel between Ring and Mickey Byrne which lasted for three quarters of the game until John Doyle took over the task of facing Christy. The crowd loved it all, and a section of Cork supporters repeatedly sang, with gusto, a verse that ended with the lines:

But the boys that beat the Black and Tans
Were the boys from the County Cork.

Christy Ring

I remember well the closing moments of the game. With normal time up, and the play entering injury time, Tipperary led by 1:8 to 1:7 and looked as if they had dethroned the Munster and All-Ireland champions. I knew that John, beside me, was suffering — 'twas etched on his face! I didn't say anything though. In circumstances like that you don't. Then in a twinkling it all seemed to happen. Ring got possession on the left wing and, having evaded tackles, floated the sliotar goalwards. From where I was it seemed to be going wide. Tony Reddan in the Tipperary goal had it covered but as he caught it, it bounced off his chest into the path of the ever-vigilant Paddy Barry who finished it by putting it into the net. Following the puck out, a twenty-one-yard free to Cork was awarded and Ring pointed it. Rebel Cork were in ecstasy. The referee blew full time; it was a Tipperary nightmare — the scoreboard read: Cork 2:8; Tipperary 1:8.

Ring had blasted a twenty-one-yard free into the net early in the second half; he made the second goal; he contributed points; he was Tipperary's tormentor-in-chief.

There was even more of a spring in John's step as we headed back to the car after the final that day. I knew that, despite a semi-final clash with Galway still to come, his thoughts were now fixed on Croke Park on the first Sunday in September.

Victory shortened the journey home. We travelled to Killorglin via Killarney where there was a stop to celebrate — no breathalyser in those days — whiskey for John and Mick and red lemonade for me.

Ringing in my ears was the chant of an elated group of Corkonians as we left the Gaelic grounds:

Toscanini for good music
Kathy Barry for crubeens
— And Ringey for goals.

Many years later, writing in *The Spirit of the Glen*, Christy had this to say:

'My hurling days are over — let no one say the best hurlers belong to the past. They are with us now and better yet to come.'

Christy was a hurling phenomenon. In an inter-county career that lasted almost a quarter of a century (1940–1963) he had the following major achievements:

8 All-Ireland medals — including four in a row (1941–44)
    and three in a row (1952-54)
4 National League titles
18 Railway Cup victories with Munster
12 county titles with Glen Rovers
9 Munster titles.

Christy was born on 12 October 1920. He died on 2 March 1979.

ALL-IRELAND FINAL CONTROVERSIES

In the early years of the GAA, controversy surrounded many of its games. In those days, even All-Ireland finals weren't immune to this phenomenon. Controversies took on various forms — objections, counter-objections, abandonment, walk-offs, refereeing and umpiring disputes.

These were all part and parcel of the growing pains associated with a National movement that 'swept the country like a prairie fire'.

Curiously, the Association's success caused it management problems, for the GAA was in many cases in the hands of enthusiastic but inexperienced people.

This chapter deals with some of the more major disputes associated with All-Ireland finals from the early days of the GAA.

1890

The year 1890 opened, as its predecessor ended, with Gaelic fire on the wane, and bad became worse as the year advanced. The governing body made efforts to carry on, but met with disloyalty, and were ignored in parts of the country. Kerry, Limerick, Waterford and Cork endeavoured to keep the flag flying in Munster. Tipp. were silent for the reason that: "inch by inch, and step by step, her hurlers and footballers were obstructing and resisting the wrath and power of ruthless landlordism." In the championships, Cork won a double triumph over Wexford though the football final was not played until the year 1892.

from *Tipperary GAA Story* by Canon Philip Fogarty

Cork, represented by Aughabullogue, and Wexford, represented by Castlebridge, reached the All-Ireland hurling final of 1890. They faced each other in Clonturk on 16 November of that year. It was a 21-aside contest and was played in the era when no number of points equalled a goal.

At half-time, Cork led by 1:3 to 0:1 and there had been no indication in the first half of what was about to unfold. As the second half progressed, a Wexford rally produced 2 goals and 1 point within a short space of time. That left the score standing at: Wexford 2:2; Cork 1:6. Wexford were ahead by virtue of goal superiority. Then the trouble started. The Cork men left the field alleging rough play by their opponents.

In a fascinating article which appeared in the Wexford publication, *Comóradh an Chéid*, Larry Larkin takes up the story:

> ... *the trouble started when a Cork man lay down and started to moan and a second player followed suit. The Wexford umpire made out they were faking injuries, but the referee would not give a decision, but he (Sheehy of Limerick) advised the Central Council to award the match to Aughabullogue because of the roughness of the Castlebridge men. He said that seven of the Cork men had to retire.*
>
> *The Wexford people thought it was an absurd decision by the referee who did not censure anyone while the game lasted. However, Cork were awarded the match....*
>
> *The hurling match was awarded to Cork on a 3/2 majority. The three who voted that way had not seen the match. The two who had — Martin O'Neill, grandfather of Martin from Ferns, and T.J. Whelan, Queen's University, who wanted the match replayed — had seen the tie. The Castlebridge umpire at the match went to attend the meeting but he was not allowed in.*
>
> *Ned Daly, captain of the Castlebridge team, was quoted as saying that if hurling matches could be won by lying prostrate on the ground, groaning and feigning injury, the practice of science for the game was quite unnecessary. He added, that both teams had a full complement of players when they scored their second goal and that two of their players were injured, 'but their courage did not fail them'.*

(You can read more about 1890 in the chapter 'Unique Senior Doubles' later in this book, page 159.)

1892

In 1892, only three teams participated in the All-Ireland hurling championship. It was a year in which political considerations dominated — a bitterly contested general election and the ongoing Parnell controversy.

In the Munster championship, Cork (Redmonds) defeated Kerry (Kilmoyley) by 5:3 to 2:5. Meanwhile in Leinster, Dublin (Davitt-Faughs) got a walk-over and so became unopposed champions of that province. No teams participated from either Connaught or Ulster that year.

The 1892 All-Ireland final took place at Clonturk Park, Dublin, on 26 November 1893, with Dan Fraher, of Dungarvan, in charge of the whistle.

Up to half-time the match was goal-less and Cork were leading by 4 points to nil. Play resumed and each side took a goal apiece. Controversy then followed, some 10 minutes from the end, when Cork secured a second goal that Dublin subsequently disputed. However, the referee awarded the goal and so the score stood at Cork 2:4; Dublin 1:1. The Dublin team then left the field and Cork were awarded the match.

P.P. Sutton, writing in *Sport* reported the match as follows:

At times the play was brilliant and at others correspondingly dull. It was scarcely up to the standard of what would be expected in the final tie for All-Ireland. There was a good deal of missing on both sides, and the combination was also faulty.

This was the first All-Ireland final where the teams played with seventeen aside. It was Cork's second title and the victorious team read:

W. O'Callaghan (Captain), J. Kennealy, M. Cassidy, J. Keegan, J. Leahy, M. Sheehan, C. O'Callaghan, D. Halloran, Tom Irwin (afterwards Secretary, Cork County Board), J. Conway, J. O'Connor, W. O'Connor, D. Scannell, J. Cashman, D. Coughlan, D. Drea, D. Buckley.

1893

In many respects the following year, 1893, wasn't much different from 1892. It opened with the GAA in a state of considerable disarray. Only three counties, Dublin, Cork and Kerry sent delegates to the annual convention in Thurles. Not many teams participated in the competitions and, again, there was no Connaught or Ulster championship. Cork (Drumtariffe), following a walkover from Kerry, became Munster senior football champions that year and reached the All-Ireland final unopposed.

In Leinster, Wexford (Young Irelands) defeated Westmeath (Mullingar). They then met Kilkenny in the Leinster final. The game was unfinished with Kilkenny leading by 0:5 to 0:1 at half-time. Alleging rough play on the part of the Wexford men, Kilkenny refused to play the second half of the match. Wexford took the field and remained there for half-an-hour. They were awarded both the match and the Leinster title.

The Young Irelands team that represented Wexford in 1893

The 1893 All-Ireland football final was to be played at Ashtown Trotting Grounds, on 24 June 1894. However, ground conditions were so appalling that the game was transferred to the Phoenix Park. This involved uprooting and transferring the goalposts. One can only wonder how the venue was ever chosen. There must have been no advance inspection. When the teams arrived they found that the grass was high, the ground pockmarked and there was lots of animal dung throughout the field.

At half-time, at the Phoenix Park, Wexford were beating Cork by 1:1 to 0:1. It had been a rough physical contest up to that point and there was more of the same to follow in the second half. Then, with just over a quarter of an hour of the match left to play, it was alleged that one of the Currans of Wexford was deliberately knocked to the ground and kicked in the head by a member of the Cork team, while the ball was 30 yards away.

The crowd then invaded the pitch and there was a general mêlée. When order was restored the referee, Mr T. Gilligan of Dublin, allowed a cooling-off period of 5 minutes. He then ordered that substitutes replace both the injured Wexford player and the Cork man who attacked him.

Cork refused this arrangement and left the grounds. The referee waited for a further 10 minutes for them to come back, but they failed to return. He then awarded the game to Wexford and Central Council upheld his decision.

Celebrations in Wexford were described as follows in Wexford's *Comóradh an Chéid 1884-1984*:

> *The victory set Wexford alight and when Young Irelands arrived back in the premier town, they were given a heroes' reception. A special Mass was celebrated in the Church of the Immaculate Conception, Rowe Street, and prior to that members of all the town's GAA clubs and football fans carried Young Irelands players shoulder high from the Redmond Monument to the Church.*
>
> *Later, four barrels of stout were consumed by deserving throats at the Young Irelands Headquarters in Selskar Street ... The Temperance Hall.*
>
> *That team which achieved a historic first for Wexford was: Tom (Skull) Hayes, (Capt.), Jack Bolger, Paddy Curran, John Quinn, John Doyle, John O'Neill, Nick Lacey, John Phelan, Mick Curran, James Malone, Tom Redmond, William O'Leary, Frank Boggan, Andy Furlong, Tommy and Jack O'Connor and T. Redmond (goal).*

The hurling final was played at the same venue on the same day. In contrast to the football final, it was a controversy-free match and Blackrock, representing Cork, had a runaway victory over Leinster champions, Confederation of Kilkenny. It was Cork's third title and the referee was J.J. Kenny, of Dublin.

1894

The All-Ireland football final of 1894 ended on a controversial note. The details surrounding the affair were dealt with in depth in my previous book *Off the Field and On* (Wolfhound Press, 1999) in the chapter entitled 'The All-Ireland Football Final Draws'.

The title was awarded to Dublin when Cork refused to engage in a third encounter. They had been leading by 2 points in the closing minutes of the second game, in Thurles, when Dublin refused to continue.

Thus did Dublin record a third All-Ireland football victory and maintain 100 per cent success rate in All-Ireland finals up to that time. The two previous ones had been in 1891 and 1892 with wins over Cork and Kerry, respectively.

An interesting feature of all three of these wins was that Dublin were led by the same captain, John Kennedy. He was the first to achieve such an honour.

Another player, Sean Kennedy, bettered his Dublin namesake by leading his native Wexford to All-Ireland football success in successive years in 1915, 1916 and 1917.

1910

In 1910, football fans were looking forward to a great All-Ireland final between Kerry and Louth. The previous year, these teams had served up some delightful high-class football with All-Ireland victory eventually going to Kerry on the score of 1:9 to 0:6. The records show gate receipts of £317:3s:6d on that occasion — a respectable amount for the time.

It is worth looking at some of the encounters involving both teams, in the 1910 campaign, that led to their qualification for the final.

In the first round, in Munster, Clare, Kerry and Cork accounted for Limerick, Waterford and Tipperary respectively. Kerry then beat Clare in the Munster football semi-final at Limerick. Following that, in a close low-scoring game, they defeated Cork in the Munster final at Cork Athletic grounds. It was a great exhibition of football that ended on the meagre score of 0:4 to 0:2. (It is interesting to note that the previous year Kerry lost at the same stage to Cork on the score 2:8 to 1:7. However, following an objection by the Kerrymen, a replay was ordered. This time the result was reversed and Kerry took the victory by 1:6 to 0:6.)

Kerry then went on to beat Mayo, by 1:7 to 0:4, in the All-Ireland semi-final at Tuam, on 21 August 1910.

The Leinster final of 1910 turned out to be one of the finest football games of the year. Scores were at a premium. Louth registered three points over the hour. Their opponents, Dublin — who had already beaten Ulster champions, Antrim, by 3:5 to 0:2 in Dublin, on 2 October — failed to raise a flag. Sliabh Ruadh reported that Carvin, Markey, Brennan and Byrne were outstanding for Louth. In an earlier game Louth had beaten London by 3:4 to 2:2 in Dundalk, on 11 September 1910.

Thus the scene was set for a repeat of the 1909 final. It would be Kerry's sixth final. Up to that time their All-Ireland record stood at three wins, two losses; and was as follows:

1892 Kerry (Laune Rangers) 0:3; Dublin (Young Irelands) 1:4

1903 Kerry (Tralee Mitchels) 0:11; London (Hibernians) 0:3

1904 Kerry (Tralee Mitchels) 0:5; Dublin (Kickhams) 0:2

1905 Kerry (Tralee Mitchels) 0:5; Kildare (Rosebery) 1:7

1909 Kerry (Tralee Mitchels) 1:9; Louth (Trodaghs) 0:6.

On the other hand, Louth would be appearing in their third final, and from their two previous appearances, they had no win to their credit. The results from these two matches were as follows:

1887 Limerick (Commercials) 1:4; Louth (Young Irelands) 0:3

1909 Kerry (Tralee Mitchels) 1:9; Louth (Trodaghs) 0:6.

Unfortunately, the eagerly awaited clash of 1910 fixed for 13 November never materialised. The source of the dispute was unique and unusual.

From enquiries I have made it seems that negotiations between the Kerry County Board and the Great Southern Railway Company regarding travel facilities for players and supporters of the Kerry team formed the root of the problem.

The GSR — confidently expecting that their offer would be accepted — would give only 20 tickets, at a negotiated price. These were for the team itself, who were making the journey to Dublin on the eve of the match. They refused to provide extra carriages at a reduced rate for the supporters of the team. On hearing this the team refused to travel.

We can only speculate that if Kerry had been in search of a first All-Ireland title they might have travelled. As it was, Kerry, represented by Tralee Mitchels, had in the recent past, 1903, 1904 and 1909, captured three titles.

There was widespread disappointment throughout Ireland at the news — fans had been expecting a classic.

Louth were awarded a walk-over but the coffers of the GAA suffered considerably. It was the first and, up to the time of writing, only walk-over conceded in the history of the All-Ireland senior football championship.

Sundry

The hurling walk over of 1911 conceded by Limerick to Kilkenny and the football final fiasco of 1925 were dealt with in detail in my previous book *Off the Field and On* (Wolfhound Press, 1999).

With the passage of time, better organisation, improved structures and greater discipline have all led to the virtual elimination of major controversies from Gaelic Games.

The most celebrated case of recent times was the All-Ireland hurling semi-final replay of 1998 between Clare and Offaly. Clare won that match by 1:16 to 2:10 but referee Jimmy Cooney blew the final whistle too early. A second replay was ordered and this time Offaly won by 0:16 to 0:13, in Thurles. This incident is also covered in *Off the Field and On* (Wolfhound Press, 1999).

The Glamour and Glory of the Purple and Gold

What's the news, what's the news
Oh, my bold Shelmalier.

It isn't widely known that at the time of the famine in the 1840s, hurling was almost extinct. It had survived in only three isolated pockets. One of those was the Castlebridge-Blackwater area of County Wexford. The other two were in the Gort-Ardrahan area of County Galway and the Aglish-Carrigaline area near Cork City.

Possibly as a result of hurling's survival in the first of these areas, Wexford were very much to the fore in both hurling and football in the early years of the GAA. They won a Leinster double in 1890 but lost both All-Ireland finals to Cork — the hurling final defeat occurring in somewhat controversial circumstances.

In the nineteenth century, Wexford contested two more hurling finals, but without success. They lost to Kerry after extra time in 1891, and, in 1899, they fell heavily before the might of Moycarkey from Tipperary: 3:12 to 1:4.

Football Glory

Wexford fared better in the early football championships. In the 1893 final they were leading by 1:1 to 0:1 at the three-quarter stage of the

The Wexford team of 1955

game. At this point their opponents, Cork, refused to continue play and Wexford were consequently awarded the title. It was the model county's first All-Ireland crown.

The glory days of Wexford football stretched from 1913 to 1918 inclusive. In those years they won six successive Leinster titles. They became the first four-in-a-row title holders, when they took the All-Ireland crowns of 1915, 1916, 1917 and 1918. They were without peer in the whole land. They were captained for four successive years — 1914 to 1917 — by Sean Kennedy, one of the greatest dual players of Gaelic games. No other player has led his county to three successive All-Ireland titles.

Wexford's All-Ireland football victories from that era were:

1915 v Kerry — 2:4 to 2:1

1916 v Mayo — 2:4 to 1:2

1917 v Clare — 0:9 to 0:5

1918 v Tipperary — 0:5 to 0:4.

The following nine players played in all four finals:

Gus Kennedy, Paddy Mackey, Tom Murphy, Tom Doyle, Aidan Doyle, Jim Byrne, Martin Howlett, Rich Reynolds and Tom McGrath.

Sadly, 1918 marked the end of the great days of Wexford football though Wexford took Leinster titles in both 1925 and 1945. That was it; and, if hindsight were foresight, 1945 might well have seen the Sam Maguire Cup come to Wexford for the first time — but it didn't. In winning the Leinster senior football title in 1945 Wexford showed themselves throughout the provincial campaign to be a very formidable force. Then came a fatal, if well-intentioned decision by the mentors and management. The team was taken to Rosslare Harbour for two weeks' collective training in preparation for the All-Ireland semi-final against Cavan; but two weeks was too long. Removed from their normal routine, a feeling of monotony set in amongst the players and they lost their edge. They were stuck to the ground against Cavan and lost the match by 1:4 to 0:5.

Hurling Glory

In 1910, Wexford hurlers won the All-Ireland crown by beating Limerick. Their next appearance in the final followed in 1918, but resulted in a heavy defeat at the hands of a more powerful Limerick side. After this the county's hurling went into decline for a number of years. Happily, for Wexford hurling, and hurling lovers, there was a renaissance for the county in the 1950s. It was universally welcomed.

It is worth taking a look at the background against which Wexford hurlers came to prominence in the middle of the twentieth century. The first sign of hope came in the Leinster semi-final of 1944. Wexford, with Railway Cup players, Joe Bailey and Nicky Rackard prominent in their ranks, defeated Kilkenny, for the first time in 36 years, before failing to Dublin in the Leinster final. However, it was a hopeful sign of things to come.

While Nicky Rackard was at UCD and playing on Leinster Railway Cup teams he rubbed shoulders with other inter-county players. That, coupled with the talent he saw coming to the surface in Wexford, led him to express the following view, in his family home in Rathnure one day in 1949: 'Do you know what? It's going to happen not far from now, maybe in a few years' time — we will be All-Ireland champions.' His brother, Billy, had listened carefully and hoped that he would be part of it himself.

A giant step towards glory was taken in 1950. Victories over Offaly and Laois brought Wexford face to face with Kilkenny in the Leinster final at Nowlan Park. Their one-goal defeat, of 3:11 to 2:11, wasn't without controversy. A ball that was whipped off the goal-line by Art Foley, in the Wexford goal, resulted in a goal being awarded to Kilkenny by the referee after the umpires had expressed conflicting views. If the goal had not been given, Nicky Rackard wouldn't have had to attempt to blast a closing-minute 21-yard free into the net for the equaliser — he would have only had to tip it over the bar for the winner.

The men in purple and gold lined out in Croke Park on the first Sunday in September 1951 to a rousing reception from an attendance of over 68,000 people. Wexford were contesting their first All-Ireland final since 1918 and their opponents were Tipperary. With a wonderful sporting display Wexford captured the hearts of all Gaeldom. Inexperience saw them lose by 7:7 to 3:9, but there was no doubt that they would be back.

It took a little while, however — probably a little longer than Nicky Rackard had anticipated. Between 1951 and 1960 inclusive, Wexford contested nine of the ten Leinster finals. They won five of them: 1951, 1954, 1955, 1956 and 1960. They converted three of those Leinster wins into All-Ireland victories in 1955, 1956 and 1960.

In the same period, they won two of the greatest National League games ever played. In 1956, against Tipperary, they were down 15 points at the interval but, aided by the breeze in the second half, they gradually chipped away at Tipperary's intimidating lead, and as they did so, the atmosphere became supercharged. The final whistle brought an unforgettable victory for Wexford with the score at 5:9 to 2:14.

Two years later, against Limerick at Croke Park, on a day ideal for hurling these two counties served up a classic contest. It had the journalists searching for superlatives and John D. Hickey, of the *Irish Independent*, said it was the greatest game he had seen. Wexford carried the day by 5:7 to 4:8, having withstood a fierce final onslaught from Limerick.

The 1950s belonged to Wexford. They played and defeated all the leading teams in rousing games: Kilkenny, Cork, Tipperary, Limerick, Clare and Galway.

We may have great men
But we'll never have better ...

Wexford played a brand of hurling that suited their physique and temperament. Their game was based, largely, on lift-and-strike and catch-and-strike. Ground hurling was alien to the men of Wexford. They had a flair for the big occasion and they drew the crowds. The largest All-Ireland final attendances were recorded in the 1954 and 1956 finals against Cork — 84,856 and 83,096 spectators, respectively. The Wexford v Limerick All-Ireland semi-final of 1955 drew a record semi-final crowd of almost 60,000 people. Wexford stamped a glamour on their image that was the envy of other teams and their sportsmanship was of the highest order.

Pat Stakelum, the brilliant Tipperary centre half-back of the 1950s, expressed the view that the arrival of Wexford gave the game of hurling a fabulous lift: 'They brought something new to it. They were mighty men with a sense of fair play that was quite remarkable.'

Nick O'Donnell receives the Liam McCarthy Cup from President
Éamon de Valera

Jim English and Nicky Rackard

The late Bobby Rackard, an outstanding defender in those glory days of Wexford hurling, had this to say in my book *Giants of the Ash* (Wolfhound Press, 1991):

> *The Wexford team of the fifties earned a respect and popularity on a National basis which far exceeded that of other teams which perhaps won a lot more. This of course was due largely to their sportsmanship and the way they played the game. I am proud to have been a member of that team.*

Dermot Kelly, of Limerick, who played against Wexford and who also watched them as a spectator described them as, '... the most exciting team I ever saw'.

Leinster titles came Wexford's way in the 1960s, 1970s and 1990s and they won All-Ireland crowns in 1968 and 1996. The Wexford hurling teams of these decades were also great but those of us who remember the men of the 1950s will always associate with them especially the glamour and glory of the purple and gold.

It is worth recalling for posterity the names of those who won the All-Ireland titles of 1955, 1956 and 1960:

Art Foley, Bobby Rackard, Nick O'Donnell, Mick O'Hanlon, Jim English, Billy Rackard, Mick Morrissey, Jim Morrissey, Seamus Hearne, Paddy Kehoe, Ned Wheeler, Padge Kehoe, Tom Ryan, Nicky Rackard, Tim Flood, Martin Codd, Tom Dixon, Pat Nolan, John Mitchell, Tom Neville, John Nolan, Jimmy O'Brien, Seamus Quaid, Oliver McGrath, John Harding, Oliver Gough, Dom Aherne and Sean Power.

Tá ochtar den bhuíon uasal sin imithe ar shlí na fírinne. Imíonn na daoine ach fanann na cnuic. I bhfoireann grámhar Dé go raibh siad i gcónaí.

The Wexford All-Ireland victory over Tipperary, by 2:15 to 0:11, in 1960 left the Munstermen in a state of shock. Mick Dunne opened his report the following day in the *Irish Press* with these lines:

The Assyrian came down like a wolf from the fold,
And his cohorts were gleaming in purple and gold.

Evolution

At a meeting of the Gaelic Athletic Association held at Hayes's Hotel, Thurles, on 17 January 1885 rules for hurling and football were discussed and adopted.

The second Annual Convention was held at the same venue on Monday, 15 November 1886, and the hurling and football rules were revised on this occasion. At this time in the history of the GAA the rules differed from those of the modern games and at no stage were they perceived as being set in stone — the rules of Gaelic Games evolved over time.

In the early years of the GAA the management of the Association moved with remarkable speed as it adjusted and altered rules and practices with a view to moulding Gaelic Games into increasingly attractive products.

In so doing, they demonstrated a commendable level of insight and vision. The action they took in those early days was also a mark of the management's capacity not to shirk the responsibility of change, as well as its openness to promote progress and development. It all belied the limited level of expertise that the members of the management had accumulated up to that point in those infant years of the organisation.

The games of hurling and football, as we know them today, did not take shape fully until 1913. A series of steps was taken during the time between the founding of the Association and that year before the games emerged as they now are. These steps are worth recording.

1887

At the time of the first All-Ireland championships, in 1887, the scoring area allowed a far larger target for the scoring of points (see Figure 1). Instead of the present day 'seventy' in hurling, and 'fifty' in football, forfeit points were awarded — one forfeit point was given for an offence and five of them equalled one point on the scoreboard. At this time, no number of points equalled a goal and teams consisted of twenty-one players each. Teams were selected from members of a parish and the successful parish represented the county. A parish was defined as a district presided over by a parish priest.

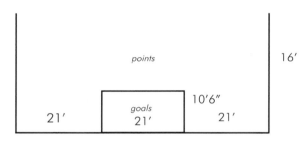

Figure 1 — *The Scoring Area 1887*

1888

At the convention to reconstruct the Association held in Thurles on 4 January 1888 (see the first chapter — 'A Skirmish in Thurles'), forfeit points were abolished and a forty-yards free (a little later changed to fifty yards) replaced them.

Also during that meeting the size of the playing pitch for hurling and football was fixed at:

Minimum — 140 yards x 84 yards

Maximum — 196 yards x 140 yards

1892

At the Congress in Thurles, on 13 January 1892, a goal was made equal to five points; the purpose of this decision was to encourage more open play as well as more long-distance attempts at scoring. This congress also heralded changes in the organisation of the teams which were reduced to seventeen players. In addition, county champions, when representing the county were, if they so wished, allowed to select players from any of the other clubs in their county.

1896

By 1896 further changes were before Congress, which was held in Thurles on 10 May of that year. The value of a goal was reduced to three points and the scoring area was reduced as illustrated in Figure 2 below. Also the height of the crossbar was reduced from 10 feet 6 inches to 8 feet, a height at which it has remained to the present day.

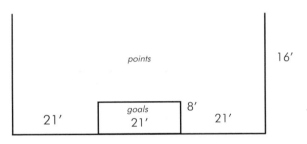

Figure 2 — *The Scoring Area 1896*

1901

Five years later, in 1901, Congress made further adjustments in the scoring area. The diagram below (Figure 3) shows that the area within which scores could be registered was reduced from 63 feet to 54 feet. This change left the goalkeeper with 3 feet less to guard along the goal-line and a total of 24 square feet less in the goal-scoring area.

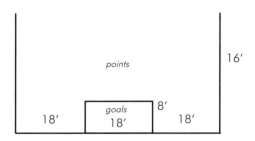

Figure 3 — *The Scoring Area 1901*

1903

As one studies those early formative years of the GAA, it becomes clear that, on a regular basis, very close consideration was being given to the development of the games — particularly with reference to the scoring area. In 1903, just two years after the last alteration, the scoring area was again the subject of change. It was now reduced to 45 feet in width, as this diagram shows:

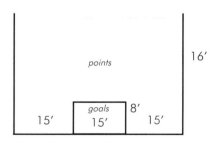

Figure 4 — *The Scoring Area 1903*

1910

The year 1910 ushered in radical changes that paved the way for the modern-day games of hurling and football:

- the side posts and the soccer-style goal-scoring area were abolished
- two uprights, 21 feet apart and 16 feet high with a cross-bar located 8 feet from the ground, formed the new scoring area: goals beneath the cross-bar; points above the cross-bar.
- nets were introduced behind the goal-scoring area
- a parallelogram 45 feet x 15 feet was located in front of goal. This area was often referred to as 'the square'. Goals scored were only allowed provided attacking players were not therein before the arrival of the sliotar or football.

Little wonder, then, that in the hurling final of 1910 points were at a premium — only two in the entire hour. As against that, 13 goals were scored. For the next dozen years or so, it was the exception rather than the rule for the number of points scored in a hurling final to exceed the goals scored — prior to 1910 the reverse had been very much the case.

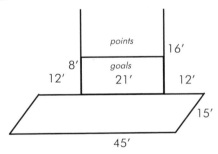

Figure 5 — *The Scoring Area 1910*
The parallelogram in front of the goal was introduced in 1910. Goals were only allowed provided attacking players were not therein before the arrival of the sliotar or football

1913

The year 1913 — 29 years after the foundation of the GAA and 26 years after the first championships — saw the final touches put to the structure that has given us the modern-day game: teams were reduced to 15 a side.

The 1970s

At the time of writing, the most recent change to the games of hurling and football had occurred in the mid-1970s. At that time, a second parallelogram measuring 21 yards x 14 yards and incorporating the smaller parallelogram, was introduced. Personal fouls, as distinct from technical fouls, committed within that area, led to a penalty in football (only one player defending the goal) and a semi-penalty in hurling (only three players defending the goal).

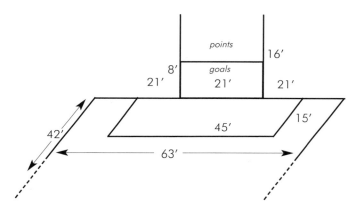

Figure 6 — *The Scoring Area mid-1970s*

Over the years, other aspects of our games also changed —change is the key to vibrancy, attractiveness and survival. I have in mind the shoulder charge; the abolition of the frontal charge on the goalkeeper; the elimination of the third-man tackle and the controls associated with the personal foul as distinct from the technical infringements. Such adjustments are indicators of the vigilance and good management that will ensure our games remain highly attractive spectacles in an ever-changing world.

THE WON-AND-LOST HURLING FINAL — 1905

The circumstances surrounding the decision — by a four-to-three majority — to replay the 1905 final were unique. Never before, or since, has there been a similar occurrence, nor is there ever likely to be again.

In the 1905 Leinster championship Kilkenny set about defending their 1904 All-Ireland crown (their first title) when they faced Wexford in the first-round match, in Athy. Kilkenny took the victory on the score of 4:10 to 1:5. Their next game was against Offaly, in the Leinster semi-final, at Jones's Road.

In that game:

> *Kilkenny looked the All-Ireland champions they were. A superb defence kept the challengers at bay, while Jer Doheny, Martin Lalor and Tom Murphy picked off telling scores, despite Herculean efforts by Offaly full-back Jack Teehan.*

Kilkenny were then nominated to represent Leinster against Lancashire, who were representing England. Before a very small attendance at Jones's Road, on 5 August 1906, Kilkenny had an easy victory with a score of 2:21 to 0:5.

Dublin were their opponents in the 1905 Leinster final and it is interesting to note that, on the Dublin side of the draw, the following qualifying results emerged:

Antrim 3:16; Glasgow 3:11

Dublin 3: 8; Laois 0: 7

Dublin 5: 8; Antrim 1: 9.

(Scotland, like England had been in 1900, was made a province of Ireland in 1905, for the purposes of the GAA.)

There was nothing novel about a Kilkenny v Dublin Leinster final; it was the tenth such meeting between these teams since the championships began. However, the results weren't always clear-cut. In 1893, for example, Dublin conceded a walk-over. In 1896, after Dublin had won 1:8 to 0:6, an objection followed and a replay was ordered. Dublin then confirmed their superiority with a decisive victory by 4:6 to nil. Again, in 1903, there was controversy. This time the game ended in a draw: 1:5 each. The Dublin goal was disputed and Kilkenny were awarded the match.

The 1905 Leinster final was played in Wexford. Tom Ryall in his book, *Kilkenny — The GAA Story 1884–1984* (The Kilkenny People, 1984), described the game, briefly, as follows:

The crowd was small and the weather wretched. Despite the bad conditions it was a great game. Kilkenny led at half-time by 1:3 to 0:1. They eventually won by 2:8 to 2:2. Two youthful players who got special mention were Dan Kennedy and Tom Kenny.

In Munster, Cork beat Waterford with a runaway victory of 4:13 to 0:2, on 12 May 1906; in Dungarvan. Their next outing was in Kilmallock on 28 October against Tipperary. The game drew a huge crowd. Rivalry between the opposing teams and their supporters was very keen. One wag remarked that 'all of the turf in Moycarkey wouldn't warm one crowd to the other'.

Tipperary dominated the first half and deservedly led at half-time by 2:4 to 0:3. The second half — or as much of it as was played — was full of thrills. Hurling with rare abandon, the men from the rebel county scored a second goal at the end of the third quarter, bringing the scoreline to 2:4 to 2:3. However, the Tipperary goalie protested. He maintained that the ball had gone over the end-line and had been brought back by a Cork forward before the score had taken place; therefore, the goal should be disallowed. However, his plea fell on deaf ears and the referee allowed the goal to stand. Pandemonium followed — there was no more hurling. Following an investigation, the game was re-fixed for Fermoy. Tipperary refused to travel and thus made their exit from the competition.

Following this, Limerick were comprehensively beaten by Cork in the Munster final, which was played in Tipperary, on 12 February 1907. The final score was Cork 7:12; Limerick 1:4. It was Cork's fifth Munster title in succession. They subsequently had similar successes between 1975 and 1979, and 1982 and 1986. No other Munster county had ever won five Provincial hurling titles in a row. Their Munster victory was followed by an All-Ireland semi-final win over Galway by 5:13 to 0:4.

So the scene was set for a Cork (St Finbar's) v Kilkenny (Erin's Own) confrontation in Tipperary on 14 April 1907. Cork wore blue jerseys while Kilkenny had donned an assortment of colours. It was the teams' third time meeting in a final. Prior to this they had taken one victory each — Cork in 1893 and Kilkenny in 1904. Only the gods knew the strange outcome that fate had in store for them in the 1905 championship.

Absent from the Kilkenny line-out was Patrick 'Fox' Maher, their outstanding goalie. He had indicated retirement after the 1904 final and was sorely missed, particularly in the first game of the 1905 final.

Years later, after Patrick Maher's death, 'Carbery' had this to say about him:

Through the years when Munster was still dominant with successive champions from Tipp. Cork and Limerick, Kilkenny was a growing danger and "Fox" Maher was the menace to the conquering men of the South. Tall, square, well turned; a hurler to his finger tips, his good looking countenance typified the hurling type such as Sean Keating or Jack Yeats would love to paint. A grand natural striker off either hand, he never dallied in possession. He could hold up the most formidable group of attackers with his wide shoulders, bony hips and bold courage. He could drive ground balls a whole field's length. Down Kilkenny way 'Fox' Maher was a personality — a hurler for all to copy, a stylist for all to study. He was on a hurling plane of his own; the greatest back and goalkeeper of the Renaissance which marked the border centuries. What Mikey Maher was to Tipp. 'Fox' of that powerful Celtic Clan of Ormonde was to Kilkenny. At Croke Park he was a familiar figure with 'Drug' Walsh and Rochford and Sim Walton — still the same quiet gentle 'Fox' Maher that the hurlers revered. 'Dia go deo leis'.

In the final, Kilkenny conceded three early goals which put them under immense pressure and, in the end, they lost by a narrow margin

— 5:10 to 3:13. It had been a superb game of hurling played in
brilliant sunshine before an attendance of about 10,000 people. It is
recorded that a goal-puck by Jim Kelliher of Dungourney hopped
once and went over the bar for a point for Cork without any player
touching it.

After the game, it came to the notice of Kilkenny that Sonny
McCarthy, the Cork goalkeeper, was a British army reservist. As such,
it was held that that rendered him an illegal player and an objection was
subsequently lodged.

Cork countered by objecting to the presence of Matt Gargan (one
of the outstanding hurling men of his day) on the Kilkenny team. Cork
claimed that he had played for Waterford in the Munster championship.
This fact was admitted by Kilkenny; no doubt, not too difficult to
prove, since Cork had played and defeated Waterford earlier in the
championship.

When the cases were heard a replay was ordered by Central Council.
It took place in Dungarvan, on 30 June 1907, before a crowd estimated
at 10,000 spectators. The replay failed to live up to the excitement and
high standard of the first game. Kilkenny took the victory by what was
seen as a somewhat sensational score margin as Cork were perceived as
being well-nigh invincible at that time. So Cork, who no doubt had
celebrated well on the afternoon of 14 April, had their seventh crown
snatched back from them. For Kilkenny, it was a case of 'The prize we
sought is won'.

Paddy Mehigan ('Carbery') was in the Cork ranks that day. He must
have felt that he wasn't destined to win an All-Ireland hurling medal at
all, having been on the London side which lost to his native Cork in the
1902 final.

Kilkenny's man-of-the-match was Jimmy Kelly who had had a field-
day with a personal score tally of 5:2. Not far behind him was the
stalwart defender, Jack Rochford, who had a superb game at full back.

The final score was, Kilkenny 7:7; Cork 2:9. The Noresiders had
retained their crown — their second title and their first two-in-a-row.
Great days lay ahead for them.

The victorious Kilkenny team were as follows (as per 'Sliabh
Ruadh'):

Eddie Teehan (goal), Sim Walton, Jack Hoyne, (Tullaroan), Jim Lawlor, Martin Lawlor, Jack Rochford (Three Castles), J. Grace (Clonmatuohy), D.J. Stapleton (Captain), Dan Kennedy, J.J. Brennan, Paddy Lanigan, Tom Kenny (Erin's Own), John Anthony (Piltown), Jimmy Kelly, Eddie Doyle, Dick Doyle, R. 'Drug' Walsh (Mooncoin).

M.F. Crowe refereed both games.

New York 1947
Cavan v Kerry All-Ireland Football Final

I still vividly remember the evening of Sunday, 14 September 1947. At about 8.30 p.m., dusk was falling on the land of Ireland but on the other side of the Atlantic, Kerry were playing Cavan at the Polo Grounds, New York, in the All-Ireland senior football final of that year.

Some neighbours of ours had gathered in the kitchen with us to listen to Micheál O'Hehir's broadcast from across the Atlantic. To us, it was some kind of miracle — even my late father was interested. It is the only match I can ever remember him listening to. We had an electric radio, one of the few in the parish, so barring a technical hitch we were sure of getting the entire match.

The event had received great newspaper coverage. Pictures were published of the players in their line-out positions along with a sketch of a ship and an aeroplane — most of the Kerry team went by ship and the bulk of the Cavan team flew.

Many years afterwards, in a newspaper interview, Micheál O'Hehir described the plane journey:

> *Three-quarters of the party went on the boat, because they didn't approve of flying — they were afraid of it. The flight took us 29 hours. We left from Shannon and went to Santa Maria in the Azores; we went from there to Gander; then to Boston, and from Boston to New York. Part of the reason was that there was a full plane and plenty of baggage. TWA put it to the party, sometime in the middle of the*

night, that if we left five people behind, to follow in a couple of days time, then we could fly direct to Boston. And of course nobody voted for anyone to be left behind.

On the matter of the telecommunication lines, which would convey his broadcast, he had this to say:

The arrangement was that Radio Éireann — as it was then — would look after the lines and microphones and everything, and the GAA would look after me, the commentator. On the Friday before the game I went down to the Polo Grounds to see where I was going to be sitting — and nobody knew anything about the broadcast. That evening we discovered there were no lines — Radio Éireann forgot to book them. Through the good offices of Mayor Bill O'Dwyer, Paul's brother, from Bohola, County Mayo, we got the lines eventually.

In honour of the occasion I got a heavy sheet of cardboard approximately 18 inches by 18 inches in size; I mixed flour and water to produce a paste and on the top of the cardboard I stuck the caption 'Kerry v Cavan'. On either side of this I placed the ship and the aeroplane, and beneath these I put the Kerry players' photos on the left and those of the Cavan men on the right. I thought it looked good. For the duration of the match I had it standing on the kitchen table against the wall. I kept it for quite a while after the game until, one day, I noticed my mixture of water and flour was generating white worms — my work of art had to be thrown out.

The idea of playing a football final in New York, for the entertainment of the Gaels in America, had been mooted for some time but it had never previously met with official approval. Efforts to stage the 1946 replay, between Kerry and Roscommon, in New York had failed. The question of the risk of a financial flop was at the back of many minds.

Canon Hamilton — outgoing Chairman of Clare County Board and a lifelong supporter of the GAA — made a special plea at the Association's Easter Congress of 1947. Together with New York delegates, he argued that, in the Centenary Year of Black 1847, it would be appropriate to remember the Irish exiles in America. The plea was successful and Pádraig Ó Caoimh and Tom Kilcoyne, Secretary of the Connaught Council, travelled to New York to survey the scene. They returned in mid-May and, following a report to Central Council, it was decided (on a vote of 20 to 17) that the 1947 All-Ireland final would be played at the Polo Grounds, New York.

That decision, which was not without controversy (as the closeness of the voting would indicate), added to the attractiveness and competitiveness of the remaining games in the championship that year.

In Connaught, Roscommon beat Sligo 2:12 to 1:8, and in Leinster, Meath defeated Laois 3:7 to 1:7. Up north, Cavan reversed the result of the previous year and defeated champions Antrim by 3:4 to 1:6. Meantime, down south, a Cork v Kerry meeting resulted in a two-point win for Kerry. A story is told about that win. It was a wet day and the goal-mouth area was very muddy. Referee Simon Deignan awarded a penalty to Cork with Kerry leading by two points. It was an era when play was held up if a player was injured and also a time when the referee, not the player, placed the ball for a free. A player was down and Joe Keohane, of Kerry, used the opportunity to argue over the referee's decision to award a free to Cork. As he was 'debating' with the referee, Joe was apparently resting his foot on the ball; in fact he was grinding it down into the mud. Jim Aherne took the Cork penalty but it must have been like kicking a piece of lead and Dan O'Keeffe, in the Kerry goal, easily gathered.

The semi-finals, between Cavan and Roscommon and Kerry and Meath, paved the way for a Kerry-v-Cavan final and a dream trip to New York for those two teams. Among the highlights of the trip was a reception at New York City Hall, hosted by Mayor O'Dwyer. There was also a meeting, in St Patrick's Cathedral, with Cardinal Spellman. Those present included the two team Captains, Pádraig Ó Caoimh, General Secretary of the GAA, Martin O'Neill, Secretary of Leinster Council, Sean McCarthy, Secretary of Munster Council, and Dan O'Rourke from Roscommon, President of the GAA.

At home, there was silence in the kitchen as the opening words of Micheál O'Hehir came over the radio from far, far away in New York.

That familiar and unique voice created a sense of drama, history and wonder for us all. The reception wasn't as clear as if he were broadcasting from an Irish venue but, nonetheless, it was great.

The preliminaries were a bit prolonged, 'Faith of our Fathers' was played followed by the two National Anthems. We would, of course, have felt a great sense of pride at the Irish National Anthem being played in the United States, side by side with that country's Anthem — America being a nation with one in five of its population of Irish descent. 'Faith of our Fathers' would also have sparked off emotional feelings in those days — on both sides of the Atlantic.

At last, it was time for the throw-in which was performed by the Mayor of New York, Bill O'Dwyer, a native of Bohola, County Mayo. However, we still had to wait; the great game hadn't started as this was merely for ceremonial purposes. The referee then threw the ball in for real and the game was finally under way.

Unfavourable weather had kept the attendance down to about 35,000 people and the Stadium was only half-full. It was an aspect of the trip that deeply disappointed referee Martin O'Neill, from Wexford. He was a proud Gael who deeply loved our games, a man dedicated to the work and ideals of the GAA; he also served as Leinster Council Secretary from 1927 until 1969.

The pre-match parade at the Polo Grounds, New York, 1947

Martin had been an outstanding sportsman in his day. In 1925, he won a Leinster senior football title with Wexford and followed this, in 1926, with a Leinster junior hurling medal. In handball he won the All-Ireland softball doubles in 1930 and 1931.

He also represented Ireland in the Tailteann Games of 1924, 1928 and 1932; and won Railway Cup football medals three years in a row from 1928 to 1930, inclusive.

During his days in Wicklow, Martin won a county senior football title, with Bray Emmets, in 1935. In 1936, he captained the county junior football team to All-Ireland victory.

The All-Ireland final of 1947 was his third time in charge of the whistle for such a match. He had previously refereed the finals of 1932 (Kerry v Mayo) and 1933 (Cavan v Galway). It was a strange coincidence that the winners on those occasions were now contesting the 1947 final in New York.

Early on in the game it looked as if Kerry, led by Captain Dinny Lyne, were going to cake-walk the occasion as they moved into an early eight-point lead; they were rampant all over the rock-hard pitch. Indeed, that early lead could well have been greater.

Then Cavan made some positional switches on the field, which steadied the team, and they began to work their way back into the game. Tony Tighe (they called him Tony 'Tiggy' in New York), a brilliant wing-forward, was up-ended as he swept through on a solo run. The crowd didn't like the tackle and booed (a reaction new to the Irish players) As a result of this incident some of the spectators switched their allegiance from Kerry to Cavan.

By half-time the Cavan recovery had put them into a 1-point lead and the scoreboard read: Cavan 2:5; Kerry 2:4. At home in the kitchen, we chatted about the first half during the interval as we eagerly awaited the second. From time to time crackling and atmospherics dulled the reception from the radio. Consequently, some of those listening would move to a different spot in the kitchen in an effort to get a clearer sound — all to no avail of course.

A very exhilarating second half ended in a welter of excitement with Cavan victorious on the score: 2:11 to 2:7. There was understandable delight among the players and jubilation in Breffni — this was Cavan's third title. They had many stars, but the names that still come to mind are: half-backs John Joe O'Reilly (their captain) and P.J. Duke (both of whom died very young), half-forwards Tony Tighe, Mick Higgins, T.P. O'Reilly and full-forward and place-kicker supreme, Peter Donohue who scored a total of eight points from frees. The New York press labelled him the Babe Ruth of Gaelic football.

On the Kerry team, the veteran Dan O'Keeffe was playing in his tenth All-Ireland final (13 if you include the three draws of 1937, 1938 and 1946). Dan had previously won seven All-Ireland medals and, on the day of the 1947 final, was as brilliant as he had been in his very first final, against Kildare, in 1931. Other Kerry men who caught the eye that day were Batt Garvey, Eddie Dowling, Paddy Kennedy and 'Gega' O'Connor.

As the game entered its very exciting closing stages, Micheál O'Hehir added tension to drama. At 4.55 p.m. New York time, it suddenly dawned on him that there was still ten minutes of the match to go and that air time had only been booked and paid for up to 5 p.m. He repeatedly appealed to the American authorities not to cut him off — 'just five minutes more', he pleaded. We too were on tenterhooks, lest we should miss those closing minutes of the final, and willed that his request be granted. Whether or not there was an 'Irish Connection' along the way, we never heard, but the style and nature of his appeal was such that it had the desired effect.

Martin O'Neill

Soon the match was all over and we felt as though we had listened to a piece of history. It was time for a cup of tea and lots of discussion.

On that historic occasion, the victorious Cavan team lined-out as follows:

Val Gannon (Mullahoran)

Willie Doonan (Cavan Slashers), Brian O'Reilly (Mullahoran)
Paddy Smith (Stradone)

John Wilson (Mullahoran), John Joe O'Reilly (Cornafean)
Simon Deignan (Mullagh)

Phil Brady (Cornafean), P.J. Duke (Stradone)

Tony Tighe (Castlerahan), Mick Higgins (Crosserlough)
Columba McDyer (Cavan Slashers)

Joe Stafford (Killinfere), Peter Donohue (Crosserlough)
P. O'Reilly (Belturbet).

| *Willie Doonan* | *P. Donoghue* | *J.J. O'Reilly* | *D. Lyne* |
| *Cavan* | *Cavan* | *Cavan* | *Kerry* |

A great story is told about Willie Doonan, the Cavan right full back, All-Ireland medal winner in 1947 and 1948.

On 26 September 1943, Cavan and Roscommon met in the All-Ireland senior football final which ended all square at 1:6 each.

At this time war was waging in Europe and Allied forces had landed in Italy. In their ranks was a radio operator — Private Willie Doonan — a footballer, whose ancestors belonged to the Travelling community.

As a Cavan man, the progress of the All-Ireland football final was as important to Willie as fighting the war. On that Sunday in September, Willie went 'missing' from his unit. After a search he was located — high up in a tree on a hillside — listening to his radio with which he had tuned-in to the broadcast from Croke Park. The playing of the All-Ireland football final of 1947 on foreign soil was definitely a once-off. In present times, it is impossible to envisage circumstances that would ever again lead to the 'export' of a final in either hurling or football. Given the capacity attendances at finals nowadays allied to million-pound gate receipts, it would be financial madness to embark on such a move.

THE PROVINCES

Munster

Munster was very prominent in the early days of the GAA, both on the field and off it. The town of Thurles was the scene of the inaugural meeting of the Association, and the three men most closely associated with the foundation of the Gaelic Athletic Association — Cusack, Davin and Croke — were from the counties of Clare, Tipperary and Cork, respectively.

In addition, the GAA's annual congress was held in Thurles until 1908, following which the venue was changed to Dublin.

Tipperary won the first All-Ireland hurling title with a victory over Galway, in Birr, and Limerick won the first All-Ireland football final with a win over Louth at Clonskeagh, Dublin. Michael Cusack (Clare) was the first Secretary of the GAA and Maurice Davin (Tipperary) was its first President.

Subsequently, ten Munster-men, representing all six counties of the province, were elected to the office of President:

Maurice Davin, Seamus Gardiner, Séamus Ó Riain (Tipperary)

Eamon Bennett (Clare)

Frank B. Dinneen, William P. Clifford (Limerick)

Michael Deering, Sean McCarthy, Con Murphy (Cork)

Vincent O'Donoghue, Pat Fanning (Waterford).

The Munster Council was the first of the provincial councils to be set up and was established following a meeting in Tipperary, on 14 October 1900.

Fourteen of the first sixteen hurling crowns came to Munster counties: Cork — 6; Tipperary — 6; Kerry — 1; Limerick — 1. Only Dublin, in 1889, and London, in 1901, broke the Munster stranglehold during this time.

In the same period, seven All-Ireland football titles were won by Munster counties: Tipperary — 3; Limerick — 2; Cork — 1; Kerry — 1.

Thereafter, Munster's share of All-Ireland crowns continued to be consistently plentiful. Titles in both hurling and football were won in every decade by Munster teams: Kerry to the fore in football, Tipperary and Cork leading the way in hurling.

Ten General Secretaries of the Association, including Seán Ó Síocháin and Pádraig ÓCaoimh, came from Munster.

It was Frank B. Dinneen of Ballylanders, County Limerick, who had the foresight and vision to purchase the different premises that comprise the site on which Croke Park stands so that the GAA would have its own national stadium.

Every Munster county has captured a senior hurling title and only Clare and Waterford have failed to put their name on the senior football trophy - although they did contest the finals of 1917 and 1898, losing to Wexford and Dublin, respectively, on those occasions.

Munster won the Railway Cup football title in 1927, the year of the competition's inauguration. What made the victory unique was the fact that the province was represented by fifteen Kerrymen — it was an era when Kerry produced magnificent footballers. This winning team is worth recalling:

Johnny Riordan, John Joe Sheehy, Joe Barrett, Jack Walsh,
Paul Russell, E. Fitzgerald, J. Slattery, Con Brosnan, Bob Stack,
Jackie Ryan, Joe O'Sullivan, T. Mahony,
Jas Baily, Frank Sheehy, P. Clifford.

In Railway Cup hurling, Christy Ring's achievement in winning eighteen titles with Munster, between 1942 and 1963, stands on a plane apart.

Munster All-Ireland Titles

County	Hurling	Football
Clare	3	—
Cork	28	6
Kerry	1	31
Limerick	7	2
Tipperary	24	4
Waterford	2	—
Total:	**65**	**43**

Ulster

The Ulster Council was the last of the provincial councils to be established. It was founded following a meeting of Ulster delegates at Armagh, on 22 March 1903, a little over eighteen years after the GAA's historic founding meeting in Thurles, on 1 November 1884.

When one considers the present-day strength of Gaelic football in Ulster, it is hard to believe that it was not until 1933 that a senior title went to the province of O'Neill and O'Donnell.

In the 1933 All-Ireland football final, Cavan were making their second attempt at the title. Captained by Jim Smith, they had a memorable 2:5-to-1:4 win over a talented Galway fifteen. (In 1928, Cavan had lost to Kildare by just one point.)

Prior to that, the only Ulster counties to contest All-Ireland finals had been Antrim and Monaghan.

In 1911, Antrim, represented by a Seoghans selection, defeated Cavan in the Ulster final by 2:8 to 0:4. In so doing they won their fourth of six successive Ulster titles. They then faced Kilkenny at Jones's Road on Sunday, 10 December, in the All-Ireland semi-final. Antrim were down 1:1 to 1:0 at half-time but they went on to dominate the second half and eventually won the match by 3:1 to 1:1.

In the final, played at Jones's Road, on 14 January 1912, before a crowd of 15,000 spectators, Antrim were comprehensively beaten by Cork (Lees) on the score 6:6 to 1:2. The referee was M. O'Brennan of Roscommon.

Nevertheless, it was an historic day for Ulster and the seventeen who did their duty on that occasion were: H. Sheehan (Captain), P. Barnes, J. Mulvihill, H. Keane, J. Murphy (Seoghans), John Darby, P.J. Williams, P. Moylan, C. McCurry, J. Fagan (Ollamh Fodhlas), E. Gorman, J. Millea (Mitchels), J. Coburn, J. Healy (Sarsfields), P. Meany, W. Lennon (Cuchullains), W. Manning (Dalcassians).

Less than ten months later, on 3 November 1912, Antrim were back again at Jones's Road to contest the 1912 All-Ireland final with Louth. The final got under way when the Lord Mayor of Dublin, Lorcan Sherlock, threw in the ball. The referee was Tom Irwin of Cork, and there was an attendance of over 18,000 spectators. Antrim were behind by 2 points to 1 at half-time and lost in the end, by 1:7 to 1:2.

In 1930, Monaghan emerged victorious from Ulster with a decisive win over Cavan. They caused a major shock in the semi-final when they defeated Kildare (one of the great football combinations of the time) by 1:6 to 1:4. However, the glory ended there: they met their match in the final, against Kerry, losing heavily by 3:11 to 0:2.

Another wonderful chapter in Ulster GAA history was written in 1960. Down, captained by their right half-back, Kevin Mussen, defeated reigning All-Ireland champions, Kerry, by 2:10 to 0:8. It was an absorbing final which attracted a record attendance of 87,768 people. The success was all the more meritorious when one considers that Down had won their first-ever Ulster title only the year before.

The men that took the Sam Maguire Cup, and the first All-Ireland senior football title, across the Border to the North, lined out as follows:

Eamon McKay

George Lavery, Leo Murphy, Pat Rice

Kevin Mussen (Captain), Dan McCartan, Kevin O'Neill

Joe Lennon, Jarlath Carey

Sean O'Neill, Jim McCartan, Paddy Doherty

Tony Hadden, Patsy O'Hagan, Brian Morgan

(K. Denver replaced Joe Lennon).

Eventually, Down replaced Cavan as the most successful football team in the province. Cavan won their last of five All-Ireland titles in 1952 but it wasn't until 1994 that Down's All-Ireland victory put them on a par with Cavan. In terms of All-Ireland success, Ulster's greatest decade has been the 1990s. Up to 1998, four titles — in a row — had gone north to Ulster; Down (1991), Donegal (1992), Derry (1993), and Down (1994).

However, this was the culmination of years of great effort and, down through the decades, other Ulster counties have had some close calls.

Antrim produced delightful footballing team combinations in 1946 and 1951: Armstrong, Waterson, O'Neill, Gibson, O'Hara, Gallagher, McCallin, McAteer, to name a few of those involved — great men, great names. Antrim well deserved an All-Ireland crown, at that time, but lost rather unluckily at the semi-final stage on each occasion — to Kerry by 3 points in 1946, and to Meath by 2 points in 1951.

All Gaeldom sympathised with Armagh in 1953. A record crowd of over 85,000 people saw Kerry and Armagh serve up majestic football at that year's All-Ireland final, particularly in the first half of the game. Armagh led at half-time, by 1:3 to 0:5, and were playing like potential champions. Late in the second half, with Kerry leading by two points, Armagh were awarded a penalty. To the dismay of their supporters, Bill McCorry, Armagh's left half-forward, had the misfortune to blaze the ball wide. When Peter McDermott, of Meath football fame, blew the final whistle the scoreboard read: Kerry 0:13; Armagh 1:6. Armagh were left to dwell on what might have been.

I was stationed in Killorglin at the time and was lucky enough to have a ticket for the game — they were like gold dust. Jim O'Connor, a cashier in the National Bank, where I worked, was a native of the Dingle Peninsula and an ardent Kerry fan. I gave him the ticket and he travelled by ghost train — a train that left Kerry in the early hours of the morning for the capital city. He thoroughly enjoyed Kerry's seventeenth All-Ireland victory.

Tyrone, despite capturing seven Ulster titles, advanced beyond the All-Ireland semi-final stage on only two occasions. In 1986, they were unlucky to finish runners-up against mighty Kerry in the final. At one stage, during the second half, they looked like potential winners but the power and experience of the Kingdom men proved superior in the end. Tyrone were equally unfortunate in 1995, when they failed against Dublin by the narrowest of margins.

Hurling lovers look forward to the day when the MacCarthy Cup will go North on its first visit; it is difficult to say when that will be and to whom it will go. The best bet would probably be Antrim.

Antrim reached the hurling final twice and, on both occasions, had looked good in their qualifying matches. In 1943, having dealt capably with Galway and Kilkenny, they fell heavily to a great Cork team in the final. Antrim's convincing semi-final win over Offaly, in 1989, suggested good possibilities against a re-emerging Tipperary team — but it wasn't to be. Fifteen minutes into the match, after a somewhat shaky start, Tipperary got a grip on the game and won it comfortably.

Six Ulster men — five hailing from the six counties of Northern Ireland — have been honoured with the office of President of the GAA. The first of these, Paddy McNamee, of Antrim, was elected in 1938 and held that position until 1943.

Another Antrim man, Seamus McFerran, was elected for a three-year term in 1955. Next to be honoured was Alf Murray, of Armagh, in 1964, and he was followed by Paddy McFlynn, of Down, in 1979. The most recent holder from the six counties of Northern Ireland was Peter Quinn of Fermanagh who was elected in 1991. Peter played a prominent rôle in the Croke Park development programme; he also very kindly launched my first book, *Giants of the Ash*.

The present holder of the prestigious office of President of the GAA is Sean McCague, from County Monaghan.

Ulster All-Ireland Titles

County	Football
Cavan	5
Derry	1
Donegal	1
Down	5
Total:	**12**

Sean O'Neill   *Dan McCartan*   *Brian McAteer*   *Bill McCorry*
Down   *Down*   *Antrim*   *Armagh*

J. McCallin   *Pat O'Hara*   *Sean Quinn*
Antrim   *Antrim*   *Armagh*

George Waterson   *Sean Gibson*   *Peter O'Hara*
Antrim   *Antrim*   *Antrim*

Connaught

Connaught was involved, albeit unsuccessfully, in the first ever All-Ireland hurling final when, in 1888, Galway played against Tipperary for the 1887 title in Birr.

The western province's first official link with the GAA came when Peter J. Kelly of Loughrea, County Galway was elected President of the Association in 1889. He succeeded Maurice Davin, after the vote at the 1888 Annual Convention which was held in Thurles, on Wednesday, 23 January 1889. Fellow Galwayman, Joe McDonagh, was similarly honoured in 1997. Others from Connaught who held the prestigious office were Roscommon men, Dan O'Rourke and Donal Keenan, elected in 1946 and 1973, respectively, and Mick Loftus, of Mayo, who completed his three-year term in 1985. As a medical doctor he had seen, firsthand, the devastation caused by excessive use of alcohol and he pioneered strongly against it.

The Connaught council was founded following a meeting held at Ryan's Hotel, Claremorris, on 9 November 1902. It was the third provincial council to be established.

All-Ireland titles were slow in coming to the west. The championships were almost forty years old when Galway hurlers took the MacCarthy Cup across the Shannon for the first time, in 1923. Following this, in 1925, Galway won a senior football title in rather bizarre circumstances.

Galway led the way, and continued to be the most successful county in the west. To date they have won four All-Ireland senior hurling titles — a poor return that in no way reflects their work for, and contribution to, the ancient game. Galway have also won eight All-Ireland senior football titles; their glory days having centred around their three-in-a-row success from the years 1964 to 1966, inclusive. However, few will ever forget the sense of elation and pride that gripped the county after Galway's defeat of Kildare, in the 1998 football final, which finally reversed the result of 1919.

All-Ireland senior football titles won by Galway, in 1934 and 1938, and by Mayo, in 1936, represented a high in Connaught football. This is confirmed by Connaught Railway Cup victories in 1934 (against

Leinster, 2:9 to 2:8), 1936 (against Ulster, 3:11 to 2:3), 1937 (against Munster, 2:4 to 0:5) and 1938 (against Munster, 2:6 to 1:5). Connaught had faced mighty football names from each of the three provinces and showed they could match and defeat the best. In 1933, after defeating Ulster by a goal in the Railway Cup semi-final, they failed to beat Leinster by only one point in the final, which ended on the score of 0:12 to 2:5.

Up to the time of writing this book, Mayo have won three All-Ireland senior football titles. The first was in 1936 with a win over Laois. A great panel of players won a famous two-in-a-row in 1950 and 1951. The team was captained by staunch defender, Sean Flanagan playing at left full back, ably supported by great team-mates including: Paddy Prendergast, Peter Quinn, Eamon Mongey, Padraig Carney, Tommy Langan and Peter Solon.

Roscommon became the third Connaught county to win All-Ireland senior honours. A richly talented band of players won two All-Ireland senior football titles in a row, in 1943 and 1944, with historic wins over Cavan and Kerry, respectively.

Old-timers still wonder how Roscommon let the 1946 title fall from their grasp. With about five minutes to go, Roscommon were two goals up but they had to settle for a draw with Kerry in the end. They then lost to the men from the Kingdom in the closing stages of the replay. However, the Roscommon players live on — Bill Jackson, Brendan Lynch, Bill Carlos, Eddie Boland, Phelim and Jimmy Murray, Donal Keenan, Jack McQuillan, Liam Gilmartin and Frankie Kinlough — to name a few.

Connaught All-Ireland Titles

County	Hurling	Football
Galway	4	8
Mayo	—	3
Roscommon	—	2
Total:	**4**	**13**

Neither Sligo nor Leitrim have ever had the honour of contesting an All-Ireland senior football final. Having taken the Connaught title in 1928 and 1975 Sligo advanced to the semi-final stages of the All-Ireland, only to have their hopes dashed by the men from Breffni and the men from the Kingdom, respectively. Leitrim, too, were successful in the west on two occasions and gave a very good account of themselves in the semi-finals. In 1927, in Tuam, they almost created a sensation when they ran a star-studded Kerry team to a mere 2-point difference in a game that ended Kerry 0:4; Leitrim 0:2. Their next victory in Connaught was in 1994, but they lost to Dublin in the All-Ireland semi-final.

Leinster

The Leinster council was established on 4 November 1900, just three weeks after the provincial council was put in place in Munster.

Leinster are second to Munster in senior All-Ireland successes — Kilkenny are the clear leaders in hurling while Dublin lead the way in football.

Only five of the province's twelve counties have seen All-Ireland success in senior hurling: Kilkenny, Wexford, Offaly, Dublin and Laois. Up to the time of publication of this book, Laois has only ever won a single title, away back in 1915 — poor return indeed for a county that has produced numerous outstanding artists of the camán.

Six Leinster counties have won senior football titles: Dublin, Meath, Wexford, Kildare, Louth and Offaly.

It is often overlooked that a Bray Emmets selection, representing Dublin, won the 1902 senior football title, beating Tipperary, by 0-6 to 0-5, in the All-Ireland home final and then defeating London (Hibernians), by 2:8 to 0:4, in the final.

Dublin, Wexford and Offaly have all been successful in both hurling and football. Wexford were the first county in Ireland to record a run of four successes in a row when a great football combination took the All-Ireland crowns in the years 1915-1918, inclusive.

Dublin dominated the early days of the football championship, winning eleven out of the first twenty-one titles. Indeed, they had eight victories under their belt by the time Kerry won their first crown in 1903.

Dublin were also the first Leinster county to win a senior hurling title; that was in 1889 against Clare (Tulla). They won convincingly by 5:1 to 1:6 in the times when no number of points equalled a goal. In fact, they had to play only two games to win the title. They beat Louth in the first round and then got a walk-over from Laois in the Leinster final.

Kilkenny didn't win their first hurling title until 1904. However, they then proceeded to blaze a trail of glory. In the ten-year period from 1904-1913, inclusive, they won seven All-Ireland titles; a performance that has never since been repeated by any hurling county. They also gave many immortal names to hurling lore during that era; among them: Sim Walton, Jack Rochford, John T. Power, John Anthony, Matt Gargan, Dan Kennedy, 'Drug' Walsh, the Doyles of Mooncoin — Mick, Eddie and Dick, and the Graces of Tullaroan — Jack, Dick and Pierce.

James Nowlan, of Kilkenny, was Leinster's first President of the GAA. He was elected in succession to Michael Deering of Cork in 1901 and was continually re-elected during a record period that stretched for twenty years. He was succeeded in 1921 by Dan McCarthy of Dublin.

In all, Leinster have had eleven Presidents of the GAA from six of its counties:

Patrick D. Breen and Micheál Kehoe (Wexford)

Bob O'Keeffe (Laois)

Hugh Byrne and Jack Boothman (Wicklow)

John Dowling (Offaly)

Sean Ryan and J.J. Stuart (Dublin)

James Nowlan and Paddy Buggy (Kilkenny).

Paddy Buggy was President during the Centenary year of the GAA, in 1984, when the hurling final was played in Thurles. Cork defeated Offaly on that occasion.

Paddy played county and inter-provincial hurling for many years and won an All-Ireland medal after playing at right half-back, in 1957, when Kilkenny defeated Waterford in a thriller final.

Leinster All-Ireland titles

County	Hurling	Football
Dublin	6	22
Kildare	—	4
Kilkenny	25	—
Laois	1	—
Louth	—	3
Meath	—	7
Offaly	4	3
Wexford	6	5
Total:	**42**	**44**

All-Ireland Final Appearances (up to 1999)

County	Hurling	Football
Antrim	2	2
Armagh	—	2
Carlow	—	—
Cavan	—	10
Clare	5	1
Cork	44	20
Derry	—	2
Donegal	—	1
Down	—	5
Dublin	21	35
Fermanagh	—	—
Galway	19	19
Kerry	1	47
Kildare	—	9
Kilkenny	47	—
Laois	3	2
Leitrim	—	—
Limerick	15	2
Longford	—	—
Louth	—	5
Mayo	—	10
Meath	—	15
Monaghan	—	1
Offaly	6	6
Roscommon	—	5
Sligo	—	—
Tipperary	33	5
Tyrone	—	2
Waterford	5	1
Westmeath	—	—
Wexford	17	8
Wicklow	—	—
London	4	5

Hurling — excludes the 1911 final, when Kilkenny received a walk-over from Limerick.

Football — excludes the 1910 final, when Louth received a walk-over from Kerry, and 1925 when no final was played and Galway were declared All-Ireland champions.

New York's football League Title

Here's to the Gaels of Ireland,
Their country's hope and pride.
In city or in hamlet,
By Suir or Shannon's side —
In Desmond wide or Ormonde,
Tyr-Owen or Ossory,
God save the Gaels of Ireland
Where'er their dwelling be.

'The Gaels' by Rev James B. Dollard

By the mid 1920s political stability had returned to the nation following the upheaval of the War of Independence and the unfortunate Civil War. At that time our games were growing in popularity, however, the only national competition at senior level was the All-Ireland championship.

Thus to further promote and popularise our national games a second national competition was seen as the way forward and so it was that, in 1925, the National League Hurling and Football competitions were inaugurated.

The first National Hurling League competition was conducted over the 1925–1926 season and on 16 May 1926, Cork took the title. They defeated Dublin by 3:7 to 1:5, before a huge gathering at Cork Athletic Grounds. The first National League football competition was played during the 1926–1927 season and Laois emerged victorious with wins over Sligo (after a replay), Kerry and Dublin.

In 1949, New York participated in the competition for the first time and did remarkably well. The New York hurlers almost created a sensation that year when they lost by only 2 points to All-Ireland champions, Tipperary, in the League final, on the score of 1:12 to 3:4.

The New York footballers went one better and did create a sensation — a mild one perhaps — but a sensation nonetheless.

In the League final of 1949, they faced Cavan, who had been beaten by Meath 1:10 to 1:6 in the All-Ireland final. Cavan avenged that defeat in the League home final when they beat Meath by 2:8 to 1:6. The Cavan footballers were a formidable and very experienced outfit. They had defeated Kerry in the 1947 All-Ireland final, in New York, and made it two victories in a row with their win over Mayo the following year. They also won the League title in 1948 after initially drawing with Cork.

Understandably, Cavan were favourites — their position no doubt strengthened by the fact that the game was held at Croke Park. New York, however, had to shake off the effects of their long journey as well as the fact that they would be playing at an away venue.

However, the Irish-Americans rose to the occasion in admirable fashion and made footballing history by taking the National Football League title on their very first attempt — the final score: New York 2:8; Cavan 0:12. The New York victory demonstrated both the strength of Gaelic football in America and the proficiency of those who played it.

Many people were surprised by the result. However, for some observers, who were aware of the strength of the New York team, the victory was not unexpected. They had seen the potential and ability of American teams when Kerry, reigning All-Ireland champions, toured America in the early Summer of 1927, of which Sliabh Ruadh wrote:

> *The Kerry champion footballers, under the managership of Mr Dick Fitzgerald, of Killarney, arrived in New York on May 26th, and were accorded an enthusiastic welcome, 'Down the gang-plank of the 'Baltic' they came on Monday evening their ruddy cheeks and sparkling blue eyes bringing joy to the hearts of many an Irish exile, and bidding us be of good cheer.'*

Kerry were the first Gaelic football team to cross the Atlantic to play in America and although they had had victories at Springfield, Boston and Hartford, they lost matches on two occasions. The first was at Celtic Park, New York, when they went under to New York; their second was at the Polo Grounds, New York, when before an attendance of 50,000, they had to concede to the footballing exiles yet again.

In May 1932, Mayo (Connaught champions of 1931, and unsuccessful All-Ireland finalists in 1932) went on tour of the United States. They had victories in Boston and New Jersey but, like the Kerrymen before them, they too lost to the New York team.

In the publication *GAA 100 Years — commentary by Micheál O'Hehir* (Gill & Macmillan, 1984) the famous commentator related the following in connection with the League Final between New York and Cavan:

> *I recall being involved in a radio programme which was beamed to New York from Croke Park: interviews, songs, build up to the game, commentary on the action and a previously scripted conclusion to the event. What I had written was on the lines of 'The exiles played well for most of the game, but as one would expect the Cavan team with its experience wore down the challenge and won'.*
>
> *All very fine except that New York won, and did so on merit, beating the home team 2:8 to 0:12. A copy of the script got into New York hands and John Kerry O'Donnell has never let me forget. Full marks to that New York side who played excellent football.*

The published photographs of the players appeared in one of our national newspapers together with a print of the American flag. It is interesting to note that, at that time, the flag only had forty-eight stars on it, as in those days the USA consisted of forty-eight states only.

The victorious New York team lined-out as follows:

P. O'Reilly (Dublin)

J. Quinn, T. Gallagher (Philadelphia), D. O'Connor

J. Redican (Offaly), Bill Carlos (Roscommon), E. Kenny (Carlow)

Pat McAndrew (Mayo), P. Ryan (Galway)

Mickey O'Sullivan (c) (New York), J. Hughes (New York)
F. Quinn (Galway)

P. Holly (Kerry), S. Keane (Kerry), J. Corcoran (Carlow).

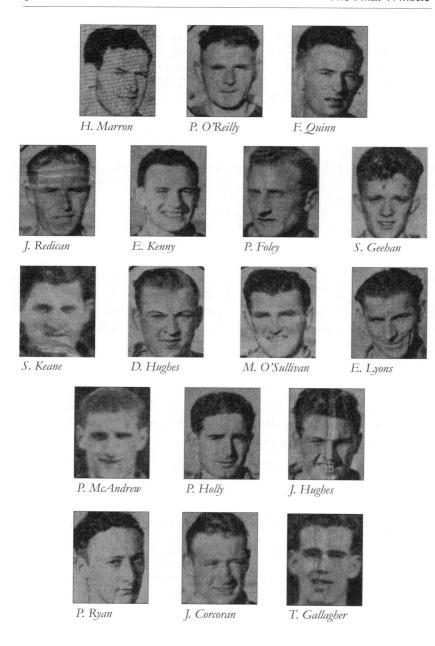

H. Marron   P. O'Reilly   F. Quinn

J. Redican   E. Kenny   P. Foley   S. Geehan

S. Keane   D. Hughes   M. O'Sullivan   E. Lyons

P. McAndrew   P. Holly   J. Hughes

P. Ryan   J. Corcoran   T. Gallagher

I Nearly Saw Mick Mackey Play

I was sitting in the side-line for the 1936 hurling final between Limerick and Kilkenny. I was eleven years old. A big Limerick man beside me, turned to me and said, did you ever see Mick Mackey, son. No, I said. Well, son, he said, you'll see him today and you'll never forget him. The parade began and Mick led the Limerick team. As he passed by me what struck me was the size of his legs — the size of his thighs. They were huge. I can still see them. He went through on a solo run and from about 21 yards stuck the ball in the net. But he didn't stop — kept going — ran in and picked the ball out of the net and handed it to Jimmy O'Connell, the goalkeeper, to puck it out. Gamesmanship, gamesmanship!!

Jimmy Heffernan, Kilkenny hurler 1944-53

I visited Mick, who was recovering from a stroke at the time, when I was writing *Giants of the Ash* (Wolfhound Press, 1991).

I was standing at the window ready to go to a funeral. Then of a sudden I spun around and fell on the floor.

That's how Mick, in his matter-of-fact way, described the onset of his stroke to me when I talked with him at his home in Ardnacrusha, a few miles outside Limerick city.

The scribes of ancient Greece and Rome would have found a dramatic way of describing the 'fall' of the immortal — and to hurling fans, indestructible — Mick. I can see them finishing their piece with the words: 'O ye gods how ye smite the mighty.'

'I'll make it big', he said, in response to my request for his autograph in the centre page of the large leather-bound journal. I nodded in approval. A special memory, I then suggested.

He gazed silently at the book for a few short seconds — pensive and reflective. It was so visible. I wondered what moments were flashing through his mind; 1933 when he had been thwarted by Johnny Dunne's goal; 1935 as he stood over the last-minute 21-yard free in rain-sodden Croke Park; 1936 and the US trip; 1936 at Thurles against Tipperary; the epic draws and replays of 1940 and 1944 at Thurles against Cork; or perhaps just those many evenings of his youth as he hurled with abandon on the local pitch. Then he said, 'It's all memories now'. He said it softly and quietly with a sense of resignation, tinged with sadness.

It made me recall those far-off days when I longed to see him in action. I had heard so much about him, he was the stuff of folklore. The stories were great: Mick, with his back to the referee, belting down the sideline on a solo run, *bas* of the hurley hidden from the referee, sliotar clasped in his left hand, supporters screaming support, opposition supporters screaming otherwise; Mick with his tongue stuck out, laughing and enjoying it all. Or the day Limerick were facing Tipperary and it was known that Mick had an injured knee. He knew it would tempt the Tipperary men. So, wisely, as a decoy, he took the field with the good knee heavily bandaged — no doubt, chuckling merrily to himself. Then there was the day that, after he had scored two goals, he turned to centre-back Con Murphy in a Munster final game against Cork, and said: 'they'll take you off any minute now'; and so the litany goes on and on.

From the mid-1940s onwards, I can remember the local hurling enthusiasts returning from the Munster championship games. Some would have cycled, others would have gone by excursion train, and as the war restrictions eased, a car-load, packed well over capacity, would head for Thurles or Cork, depending on who was playing. They would always bring back a programme of the match — in those days, generally, a simple enough production.

When Limerick would lose to Cork we would ask why, what had happened? Local wags would tell us that Mick Mackey sold the match for £40. In our youthful innocence we half believed it.

Mick Mackey leads the Limerick team out for the Munster hurling final

For days and weeks afterwards the game would be talked about and 'replayed' over and over again — after Mass, over a drink, at the creamery or in the meadows. Mick Mackey was well into the late autumn of his great career at this stage but he was still the darling of the crowd. The legs were slower but his array of tricks and dodges still remained.

How I used long to see him play. But I could get no one to take me. 'You'd get killed in the crowd', I would be told. 'You'd be walked on; there can be fierce crushing and swaying in the excitement', others would say. Even so, I would have gone, if I could have got someone to take me.

In 1945, at 33 years of age, Mick was still serving up spectacular stuff in the white heat of battle for province, county and club. It was an era in hurling of hard physical combat and hefty shouldering. A neighbouring family in the village, the Roches, cycled to the county final between Ahane and Granagh-Ballingarry at the Gaelic Grounds in Limerick. Mrs Roche's brother, Paddy Browne of Knockaderry, was playing with Granagh-Ballingarry; he was a stylish and accomplished hurler. The following day I remember her telling us that 'Paddy got a dart of a hip from Mick Mackey that sent him ten feet up in the air and I thought he'd never come down'. We loved it. It matched the stuff we learned at school about Fionn MacCumhaill and the Fianna warriors.

Mick played in 1946 and came on as a sub in the second half of the 1947 Munster championship first-round match against Tipperary. When I was told by a neighbour about the incredible reception the crowd had given Mick as he took the field I wished, like Jimín Mháire Thaidhg in our schoolbook *Is fada liom go mbead Mor*, that I was grown-up and could have been there.

Mick retired in 1948 and so ended his inter-county career, but I still didn't lose hope of seeing him play. After all, there was always the county championships.

In 1949, the opportunity came at last. I had been watching the progress of the county senior hurling campaign closely and, that year, the semi-final brought a meeting between Ahane and Croom-Young Irelands. It promised to be a humdinger as both sides had hurling stars and legendary names in their line-outs. Almost the entire county panel was involved.

The alliance of Croom and Young Irelands was an unusual one — a rural and city combination — and its sanction puzzled many people. It was suggested in some circles that a strong hurling unit was being sought in order to end Ahane's monopoly of the senior hurling championship.

Since 1931, Ahane's hurling history had been quite remarkable. They contested their first county senior title that year and defeated Croom by 5:5 to 1:4. From 1933 to 1939, inclusive, they won seven successive county titles. Croom halted their gallop in 1940 and 1941, but Ahane were back again in 1942 and, between then and 1948, took another seven such victories in a row. This gave them a total of fifteen titles in eighteen years. For good measure, they won five consecutive senior football titles between 1935 and 1939, inclusive, with basically the same personnel as they had had in the hurling championships.

However, to return to 1949; there were only two survivors from 1931 in the Ahane line-out: they were Mick Mackey and his brother John — it would be great to see them both in action. I had been dropping hints to my father for some time about how I'd like to see Mick play. By this time though, he had given up going to matches. In his younger days he had played football with his native parish in Longford and even refereed matches. The GAA's approach to the 'Ban' disillusioned him and the suspension of Douglas Hyde left him aghast and somewhat bitter. But he responded to my request and it was agreed we would go to the match at the Gaelic Grounds in Limerick. *Bhí sceitimíní áthais orm.*

The night before the match there was a discussion on Mick's career — which was a wide-ranging one. He first pulled on a Limerick jersey at the Gaelic Grounds, in Limerick, on 16 November 1930. He had gone to watch a National League game between Limerick and Kilkenny but as Limerick didn't have a full compliment of players, Mick was called upon. He was just over 18 years old at the time, having been born on 12 July 1912.

In the late autumn of 1931, Mick won his first county senior hurling honours with Ahane when they defeated Croom for the Limerick title. He won his fifteenth and last county medal in 1948.

He first lined-out for Limerick in August 1929, when their minors faced Waterford in the championship. They lost and saw the victors go on to take All-Ireland honours.

He established himself full-time on the Limerick senior team in 1932 following a win over the 1930 champions, Tipperary, in the first round of the Munster championship. It is interesting to note that Garrett Howard, who later declared for his native Limerick, played at left half-back that day for Tipperary.

The following year, 1933, Mick won his first Munster title and in 1940 he won his fifth, and last, after two hectic battles with Cork. Three of those Munster titles were converted into All-Ireland crowns — 1934, 1936, and 1940.

In 1934, Mick won his first National League medal, which Limerick clinched by their win over Dublin in the last game of the competition — a game in which Mick's brother, John, was the star of the field. It was the first of five league titles in a row for the county.

A Railway Cup medal was a highly coveted honour in those days. Mick won his first in 1934 and his last — of eight — in 1945. One of the great highlights of his illustrious career was the Limerick team's trip to America, in 1936. The team sailed across the Atlantic from Cobh on the *Manhattan*. They played and won games at Yankee Stadium and Cambridge, Massachusetts and were wined, dined and entertained like royalty. They returned home on the *SS Washington* and arrived in Cobh on the 9 June, having spent six days at sea.

In the Munster final of 1936, Mick ran up a personal score tally of 5:3 against mighty Tipperary.

Oh, how I had looked forward to seeing him in action; and there would have been the added bonus of watching Paddy Clohessy — stalwart Limerick defender of the 1930s — in action as referee. Paddy, a granite-like figure on the hurling field, came on as a sub on the Munster Railway Cup team of 1932 and from then, up to and including 1940, gave peerless performances in the centre half-back position.

We rose early on the Sunday morning and went to 8.30 Mass. It was a beautiful fresh sunny Autumn day and this augured well for the hurling game. It was now about 11.30 a.m. and everyone was in gleeful humour. We were attending to odds and ends and a light meal was being prepared for us before we headed off.

Then a telegram arrived at the house from Longford. The message was short and sad. My father's mother had died. It was one of the very few occasions on which I saw my father visibly distressed. There was, of course, a change of plans and he made preparations for the long journey that would take him right to the Cavan border.

Ever afterwards when people would ask me if I ever saw Mick Mackey hurl, I would simply reply — 'I nearly did'.

Mick was a hurling colossus — the darling of the crowd, Munster's pride and Limerick's glory.

His inter-county career lasted from 1930 to 1947.

Mick's many achievements included:

3 All-Ireland titles
5 Munster titles
8 Railway Cup medals
15 county titles with Ahane
5 National League title — all in a row in the 1930s
The 1980 Special All-star Award.

Mick was born on 12 July 1912. He died on 13 September 1982.

THE RISE OF CLARE

Clare was always a great hurling stronghold — especially the eastern part of the county — and it always produced fine hurlers. Unfortunately, All-Ireland honours — often richly deserved — tended to elude Clare teams. However, they were able to display their skills and taste success in Railway Cup games, the memories of which recall such names as Tull Considine, John Joe Doyle, Tommy Daly, Larry Blake, Jim Mullane, P.J. Quane, Matt Nugent, Dan McInerney, Jimmy Smyth, Jim Carney, Pat Cronin, Jimmy Cullinane and Seamus Durack.

However, the men of Dal Cais have a long history and it is worth tracing their fortunes from the beginning and down through the decades.

In 1889, the second year of the All-Ireland championships, Clare emerged as Munster title-holders after a bizarre campaign in that province.

In the early stages of the Munster championship of 1889, Clare (Tulla) beat Limerick (South Liberties) and Kerry (Kenmare) beat Cork (Inniscara).

The records vary as regards what took place after these two games. One account suggests that Kerry gave Tipperary a walk-over in the second round while another states that, in the final, Clare got a walk-over from Kerry.

However, this is what T.F. O'Sullivan, author of *The Story of the GAA* (1916), had to say on the matter:

Kerry were subsequently drawn against Tipperary (Moycarkey) at Limerick Junction on Friday 18 Oct., but their opponents failed to turn up, and the match was awarded to Kerry. The Central Council, however, upset the decision. Moycarkey beat Tulla Emmets (Clare) ... by 5:1 to 2:2 but the match was ordered to be replayed. The Moycarkey team refused to replay the game and Tulla were declared champions of Munster though Kerry had not been defeated.

The All-Ireland final was played at Inchicore before a gathering of about 1,500 people on Sunday 3 November 1889. Dublin, whose only game in the championship had been against Louth, defeated Clare by 5:1 to 1:6. However, this result could well have been very different. Before the match the men of Clare — all twenty-one of them — had discarded their boots and lined-out for the throw-in in their bare feet. It was to prove a fateful move. On a dry sod in the first half Clare dominated and at half-time should have been further ahead than 1:5 to Dublin's 1 goal. Then came a light shower and tragedy for Clare. On a slippery surface they couldn't hold their footing. Their control and speed and composure were all lost. Throughout the field they disintegrated as a unit — the forwards scoring only one point and the defence conceding a total of 4 goals and 1 point.

The Clare team lined-out as follows:

*Thomas Coughlan, Denis McKenna, Daniel McNamara,
John McNamara, Daniel Quigley, Daniel Moroney, Mathew O'Dea,
William Moroney, Michael Curry, Ned Curry, Patrick O'Neill (goal),
Timothy O'Connell, Michael Flynn, Patrick Vaughan, John McKenna,
Martin Russell, Patrick McGrath, Timothy Donnellan, John Moloney,
James King and Michael Kinniry.*

John McKenna emigrated to England. Martin Russell and Patrick McGrath emigrated to Chicago. John Moloney went to New Zealand where he died. Timothy Donnellan, James King and Michael Kinniry all went to America.

It was not until 1914 — a quarter of a century later — that Clare senior hurlers captured the Munster crown again. After a first-round win over Kerry, Clare went into special training for the semi-final against Limerick. The preparation paid dividends and Clare created somewhat of a sensation, taking victory on the score 4:2 to just 2 points. The way was then clear for a Munster final meeting with Cork in Thurles; and when the referee of this match — that great Tipperary hurling warrior, Tom Semple — blew the final whistle Clare became Munster champions for the second time on the score of 3:2 to 3:1.

They now set their sights on the All-Ireland crown.

Under the watchful eye of Jim O'Hehir (father of Micheál of broadcasting fame) Clare did a further three weeks' special training in Lisdoonvarna. Again, this paid off for them and on 18 October 1914 a strong, fit and well-drilled outfit outplayed Laois at Croke Park before an attendance of 12,000 spectators. Clare won the match comfortably and became the 1914 All-Ireland champions. The final score was 5:1 to 1 goal.

Brendan Considine, a student at St Flannan's College, Ennis, played at corner-forward for Clare and scored their only point. Here is how he remembered some of his colleagues from that occasion:

> They were a fine body of men. Most of them were 6ft or over. Many of the team were highly skilled in the art of doubling on the flying ball. The captain of the team was Amby Power and, at 6'4", he was the team's giant.
>
> The Dodger — that was my brother Willie — played a wonderful game in the final. He had strength and courage above the ordinary.
>
> Martin Moloney, who was better known as 'Handsome', was a beautiful player and a lovely striker of the ball.
>
> Tom McGrath from O'Callaghan's Mills was a fine full forward. He had great drive and speed. Bob Doherty from Newmarket-on-Fergus always played with determination and distinction, and he later hurled with Dublin.

Clare's next opportunity for glory wasn't to come until 1932. They had a powerfully experienced team and a first-round win over Kerry set them on the road to the Munster final. Clare's opponents were the reigning All-Ireland champions, Cork, whose line-out was littered with household names. The final whistle, at the end of a thrilling game, brought a shock result to the hurling world of the time — Clare 5:2; Cork 4:1.

However, greater drama still was to unfold at Limerick Gaelic Grounds on 14 August in the All-Ireland semi-final against Galway.

With Mick King at centre-forward in devastating form, Galway moved into a half-time lead of 13 points. They quickly increased this to a 16-point advantage early in the second half — then the inexplicable happened. Tull Considine went on a scoring rampage for Clare and ran up a huge personal tally. It brought Clare a 5-point victory and an unusual final score that read: Clare 9:4; Galway 4:14.

Thus Clare went on to the All-Ireland final meeting with Kilkenny, after two weeks' training at Mountshannon. As at the Battle of Waterloo, it was a close call. The final ended on the following score: Kilkenny 3:3; Clare 2:3. It was a hard and physical contest between fit, strong men on both sides. Clare had perhaps a greater share of the ill-luck of the day, particularly in the form of two Kilkenny goals that had a strong suspicion of 'square ball' written across them. Also, there was a perceived foul on Tull Considine that might have brought a 21-yards' free in the closing stages — but it didn't.

The Clare heroes of 1932 were: Tommy Daly in goal, who won a junior All-Ireland medal with Clare in 1914 and All-Ireland senior medals with Dublin in 1917, 1920, 1924 and 1927; 'Jumbo' Higgins; Pa 'Fowler' McInerney, who played in goal in the All-Ireland winning Clare team of 1914 and was full back on the successful Dublin team of 1927; John Joe Doyle (Captain), who, as I write (July 2000) is still hale and hearty at the age of 94; Jim Houlihan; Jim Hogan; Larry Blake; Tom McInerney, half-brother of Pa 'Fowler'; Jack Gleeson; Mick Falvey; M.Connery; Michael O'Rourke, brother of Tom who won an All-Ireland senior title with Dublin in 1927; Jim Mullane; Tom Burnell and Tull Considine.

After 1932, however, Clare's fortunes wavered. Despite a league title in the season of 1945–46, great Oireachtas displays in the early 1950s and victories over Cork and Tipperary in the Munster championship of 1955 the door to major honours remained shut.

Then in the 1970s a great band of hurlers emerged to wear the Clare jersey. They included: Seamus Durack, Jim Power, Ger Loughnane, Sean Stack, Sean Hehir, Jackie O'Gorman, Johnny Callinan, Colm Honan and Enda O'Connor — to name just a few.

For three years in a row Clare met Kilkenny in the league final — an era when Kilkenny produced some of its greatest hurlers. In the

1975–76 season Clare drew with Kilkenny in the final and then suffered a 5-goal trouncing in the replay. However, Clare put defeat behind them and took the next two league titles with the following results:

1976–77 — Clare 2:8; Kilkenny 0:9

1977–78 — Clare 3:10; Kilkenny 1:10.

They looked to be All-Ireland championship material, but disaster was to strike — twice.

During the early stages of the 1977 Munster final it seemed that Clare had the measure of All-Ireland title holders, Cork. Then tragedy. Their full back, Jim Power, was sent off. They played most of the game with 14 men and in the end, lost by only five points — 4:15 to 4:10.

The following year brought another Cork–Clare confrontation in the Munster final. Playing against a fairly stiff breeze in the first half, Clare went in at half-time with only a 2-point deficit to bridge. There was a murmur of expectation among the huge gathering of 54,981 people that suggested that Clare were about to dethrone the All-Ireland champions; but it didn't happen. For some strange reason — difficult to analyse, difficult to explain — Clare's performance dropped a gear in the second half. At full time, the scoreboard read: Cork 0:13; Clare 0:11. The Clare team and supporters felt devastated and went home wondering whether they would ever reap a hurling harvest. They had to watch with envy as Cork went on that year to complete a three-in-a-row of All-Ireland successes.

However, it's a long road that has no turning and a reversal of fortunes finally came for Clare in the 1990s — though not before they suffered moments of terrible foreboding.

Close wins in two very competitive games against Limerick and Cork augured well for their Munster final meeting with Tipperary, on 4 July 1993. Expectations were high. For Clare, the result was devastating and the defeat even more comprehensive than the final score of 3:27 to 2:12 might suggest. The county felt shattered — the future looked bleak.

In 1994, Clare avenged the Tipperary defeat of the previous year. That was progress, but they lost the Munster final to Limerick in

Thurles by 9 points. The future again looked bleak — only a soothsayer could have seen the glory that lay ahead.

At last in 1995, under the leadership of the indefatigable Ger Loughnane, Clare rose phoenix-like from the ashes of the recent past. In a brilliant campaign they defeated Cork, Limerick, Galway and Offaly. The defeat of Limerick made them Munster title-holders and a terrible psychological barrier was thereby removed. Victory over Offaly made them All-Ireland champions for the first time in eighty-one years. The celebrations were indescribable. The famous victory was watched by Tom McInerney and John Joe Doyle, surviving veterans of the 1932 final. Observing also was the great Jimmy Smyth who starred with Clare in a career that lasted almost twenty years. With the exception of 1957, he was an automatic choice on the Munster Railway Cup teams from 1954 to 1964 inclusive.

For the rest of the decade Clare served up vintage hurling — hurling in all its stern naked grandeur — against all the leading counties; it was fast, direct, varied, aggressive and absorbing.

However, in the Munster semi-final of 1996, in the sweltering heat of a June afternoon, Clare fell to Limerick in a breathtaking contest. In the closing moments of the game, after a 60-yard solo run, Ciaran Carey sent the winning point over for Limerick — 'the greatest winner ever scored'.

In 1997, Clare's fortunes returned as they secured another title. The mighty ones — Cork, Tipperary and Kilkenny - all collapsed before the power of Clare. Tipperary fell in the Munster final by 1:18 to 0:18 and then again in an epic All-Ireland contest with a final score of Clare 0:20; Tipperary 2:13 (as defeated Munster finalists Tipperary had re-entered the championship through the back-door).

The following year, in the 1998 championship, Clare played six games before bowing out under unusual circumstances at the semi-final stage. Their hurling against Cork in the Munster semi-final in the last quarter of the game was truly awesome. They overpowered Waterford in appalling weather conditions in the Munster final replay. Then came three unforgettable semi-final matches with Offaly. Those who were privileged to witness the third game, in Thurles, will never forget the occasion. It was the kind of hurling the traditionalists love — hard, direct, replete with good striking, furiously paced, fierce man-to-man combat and sportsmanship of the highest order. (Despite a valiant performance from Clare, Offaly emerged victorious and went on to meet Kilkenny in the final.)

In 1999, Clare served up more vintage hurling. Tipperary fell yet again to the men of Clare after a replay. This was followed by an epic draw with Galway after Clare had lost to Cork by only 4 points in an exciting Munster final. Clare made their exit from the championship when they lost the All-Ireland semi-final to Kilkenny by 4 points.

Clare were the team of the 1990s. They brought to that decade in hurling terms, what Limerick brought to the 1930s and what Wexford brought to the 1950s.

Bravo, bravo, Clare.

Sean Mac Mahon, anchor-man of the Clare defence, who gave many quality performances for his county in the centre-half position

Dublin's Non-Native Hurling Titles

In 1925, the rule giving players the option to declare and play for their native county was put into effect; prior to that a player could only play for the county in which he resided.

In this regard, Dublin had been a major net beneficiary up to this time. Men came to the capital from the country to join the army, the Garda Síochána, attend college and seek work in the city.

The city was awash with many brilliant hurlers and their presence there brought four All-Ireland senior hurling titles to the capital. It is interesting to note that on each victorious occasion the Dublin team met and defeated the reigning All-Ireland champions. Dublin had won their first All-Ireland title in 1889 (Kickhams beat Tulla of Clare by 5:1 to 1:6) and, when they took their second in 1917 (with a Collegians selection), it was with a team that didn't contain a single native Dubliner.

Dublin lined-out that year as follows:

*Tommy Daly, Charlie Stuart, (Clare); Mick Hayes,
Mick Neville, (Limerick); Frank Burke (Kildare); Joe Phelan (Laois);
Sean Hyde; P. Kennefick; Sean O'Donovan (Cork);
Tommy Moore (Kilkenny); Hugh Burke, Jim Cleary, Bob Mockler,
Martin Hackett, John Ryan — the captain, (Tipperary).*

The game had been in progress for only a few minutes when a facial injury caused Hugh Burke to retire. He was replaced by Brendan

Considine, of Clare, who had previously played on his native county's winning team in the All-Ireland final of 1914. Brendan was hardly on the field when he proceeded to score a memorable goal following a pass from Frank Burke. This secured Dublin's unexpected victory over the reigning All-Ireland champions Tipperary, led by the renowned Johnny Leahy, on the score of 5:4 to 4:2.

The Hackett brothers, of Tipperary, played on opposite sides in the 1917 final — Martin with his adopted Dublin and Stephen with his native Tipperary.

Frank Burke won the first of his two hurling medals that year with Dublin and later added three senior football title medals in 1921, 1922 and 1923.

'Carbery', recalling the final in an article in the *Irish Independent* in 1934, the Jubilee Year of the GAA, had this to say:

Phoenix-like from the ashes of heroes in 1916 arose a new national spirit which was to bring such rapid changes in another decade. The cultural movement gripped Schools, Colleges, and Universities through the country. University College, Dublin, Alma Mater of many patriots, took the national pastime to its bosom. Headed by Dr J.M. Ryan, a 6 foot 3 giant from the Limerick-Tipperary border, the Fitzgibbon Cup boys won the Dublin senior championship and made new hurling history....

I was one of 12,000 spectators who saw a magnificent struggle at GAA Headquarters on a bright Sunday in October, 1917. Collegians' speed was a revelation. Bob Mockler, then in his glorious prime, was heroic at centre, playing masterful hurling for the county of his adoption against his schoolmates from Horse and Jockey, Moycarkey, and Boherlahan. We looked on this well-knit Tipperary side as assured champions.

Yet they met their equals in hurling skill and peers for speed in this new-strung Dublin side.

Tom Daly (later Dr Daly of Clare and Ireland teams) early stopped hot Tipp. shots from Collison and Shelly. Mockler and Donovan at centrefield for Dublin mastered their men and sent Burke away. O'Meara cleared only for Mockler from eighty yards out to draw first blood for Dublin. Cleary and Burke forced another seventy and Mockler was dead on the mark for a second minor. Considine came on (for H. Burke injured), and the young Clare banker at once swung a deadly centre which Phelan flashed to the net. Tom Moore drove another to Phelan, who passed to Neville, and the Limerick man shot hard from close range to beat O'Meara. This sensational opening sent Dublin's strong following into ecstasies. It was a revelation in cohesive attack. When Tipperary attacked, Sean Hyde and Daly were immense. They couldn't prevent Shelly's elusive dribble, however, and he goaled promptly, raising Tipp's hopes, which were strengthened when Collison tore in for a second goal. Sean Leahy was just wide with two Tipp. frees, and half-time came with the score: Dublin 2:2 Tipp. 2 goals.

Tipp's traditional finish was anticipated when they set their backs to the sun in the second half. Leahy's fine point from a free set the scores at 7 to 8. Then came Dublin's backs' stern battle to hold their lead against the fire of the flower of Tipperary. Daly was immense. He stopped shots from all angles. His goal drives rivalled O'Meara's sailing pucks. Ryan and Hyde hurled stubbornly, sending Mockler and Considine away to place Phelan for a great shot and goal. A flying doubler of Considine brought a fourth, and when Phelan burst through for Dublin's fifth major, Tipperary were staggered.

Only for the moment, however, they rallied manfully, and Ryan was hard set to clear from Shelly, who was closely marked by Hyde. The Leahy pair fed Dwyer, however, and a great goal brought Tipp. hopes. When Darby Collison tore through a forest of Dublin hurleys for Tipperary's next point the issue was still open. In a glorious typical Tipp. late rally; their desperate forwards swept the field and goaled. It was their fourth and last major; their final effort came too late, and Collegians' training helped them to hold the impetuous forwards in a finish which will live long in memory. Dublin were in three finals through the next four years of stirring political happenings which served, amongst other momentous results, to strengthen Hurling's place in the life of the Nation.

In 1920 and 1924, Dublin repeated their All-Ireland hurling success with victories over Cork (4:9 to 4:3) and Galway (5:3 to 2:6) respectively. Again, the team contained no native Dubliners in 1920 and, as far as I can trace, none in 1924 either.

The 1924 Dublin team had the great Galway midfielder, Mick Gill, in its ranks. He created a bit of GAA history. On 14 September 1924, he was on the Galway team that won its first All-Ireland senior hurling title with a victory over Limerick, in the 1923 final. Exactly three months later to the day, on 14 December, he lined-out with his adopted

Dublin team — not being eligible to play with his native Galway. He must have had mixed feelings when the final whistle blew — joy at winning a second All-Ireland medal and a sense of regret that it should have been at the expense of his own county.

In 1927, Dublin had what was perhaps their most famous All-Ireland victory. In the final they faced reigning All-Ireland champions Cork — a great team with brilliant hurlers in its ranks. Cork were the firm favourites. However, on the day, they were facing an excellent Dublin hurling unit. With one player from UCD, two from Faughs, three from Army Metro and nine from Garda, the understanding, combination and fitness of the Dublin team were of the highest order. Dublin took a grip on the game early on and never let go. Cork struggled, but the final score was: Dublin 4:8; Cork 1:3.

The victorious Dublin team had players from a total of three provinces and six counties.

The 1927 All-Ireland Hurling Final
Dublin line-out

Tommy Daly (Clare)

Joe Bannon (Tipperary), Pa 'Fowler' McInerney (Clare)
Bill Phelan (Laois)

Ned Tobin (Laois), Martin Hayes (Limerick)
Jim 'Builder' Walsh (Kilkenny)

Mick Gill (Captain) (Galway), Jack Gleeson (Clare)

Tom O'Rourke (Clare), Dinny O'Neill (Laois)
Garrett Howard (Limerick)

Tom Barry (Tipperary), Ned Fahy (Clare), Mattie Power (Kilkenny).

Tommy Daly was the only player to take part in all four Dublin triumphs. He, together with 'Fowler' McInerney — All-Ireland medal winner with Clare in 1914 — and Jack Gleeson, subsequently declared for Clare and all three were on the team that won the Munster title in

1932. The following year, at 39 years of age, Tommy Daly kept goal for Munster in the Railway Cup.

Garrett Howard, who won his first All-Ireland medal with Limerick in 1921, was also on the 1924 Dublin winning team. He later declared for Limerick, who won Munster titles in 1933, 1934, 1935 and 1936, and All-Ireland titles in 1934 and 1936.

Before playing for Dublin, Mattie Power had been on the team of his native Kilkenny when they won an All-Ireland title in 1922. He declared for Kilkenny and added All-Ireland medals to his collection in 1932, 1933 and 1935, bringing his total, like that of Garret Howard, to five.

The 1927 All-Ireland win saw Dublin hurling enter the closing stages of a golden era as the declaration rule saw many players gradually opt for their native counties.

Mention of 1927 reminds me of a fascinating and, in retrospect, amusing piece I read in Sliabh Ruadh's *History of the GAA 1910–1930* (Kilkenny Journal Ltd, circa 1932):

> *At the Tipperary Convention for 1927 the question of Gaels attending foreign dances arose, and on a resolution proposed by Mr Mahon (Busfield), seconded by Mr Flood (Thurles), it passed that Irish dances should hold premier place in dances held by GAA Clubs. Mr Willie O'Dwyer (Boherlahan) said it was 'a terrible slur on Irish people to see boys and girls dancing imported dances from London, Paris and Timbuctoo. It was a pity the men of Easter Week died for half of them.'*

Dublin won a league title in 1929 but the All-Ireland final of 1934 was lost to Limerick after a replay. In 1938, Dublin, still with a liberal sprinkling of non-natives, including their captain Mick Daniels, won its sixth All-Ireland crown with a victory over Waterford. Sadly, it was the capital's last hurrah in the hall of fame of senior hurling titles.

Subsequently, Dublin have won Leinster titles in 1941, 1942, 1944, 1948, 1952 and 1961. They went on to contest the All-Ireland finals in those years and came nearest to success in 1961, when they lost to Tipperary by only one point on the score of 0:16 to 1:12.

To hurling lovers Dublin hurling is an enigma. The capital has the players, the clubs and the facilities. However, something is missing. If that something could be found the game of hurling would be the real winner.

MAYO'S FOOTBALL SIX-IN-A-ROW

Mayo won their first of six successive National League football titles in the 1933–34 competition. They had not lost a match in their group that year — the results from which were as follows:

v Meath 2:4 to 1:5

v Cavan 1:6 to 1:6

v Galway 2:8 to 0:3

v Louth 4:3 to 1:3.

They headed the group with a total of seven points.

In the final, they played Dublin, in Castlebar on 13 May 1934, and drew: Dublin 2:3; Mayo 1:6. The replay took place at Croke Park on 15 October and on this occasion, Mayo won by 2:4 to 1:5. The result was a harbinger of things to come. Great days lay ahead.

The 1930s was a decade during which Mayo dominated in the west. Between 1930 and 1939 they contested every Connaught final. They won seven of these — losing only in 1933, 1934 and 1938 to Galway by the slim margins of 2 points, 5 points and 3 points, respectively. In two of those years they saw Galway go on to take the All-Ireland crown: in 1934 with a 2-point win over Dublin and in 1938, when they took a famous 3-point win over Kerry after a replay.

In 1936, they won what every player dreams of — an All-Ireland title. Having drawn with Galway in the Connaught final, 2:4 to Galway's 1:7, they won the replay by 2:7 to 1:4. That victory took them to an All-Ireland semi-final meeting in Roscommon with arch-rivals, and the then kingpins of Gaelic football, Kerry. The final whistle heralded a famous victory. The Kingdom had fallen on the score 1:5 to 0:6.

For Mayo, it was sweet revenge for the agonising earlier defeats of that decade at the hands of the Kerrymen. In 1930, Mayo had lost the All-Ireland semi-final to them by 1:9 to 0:4, in Roscommon. The following year, in Tuam at the same stage of the championship, they failed by 1:6 to 1:4, and in 1932 they must have wondered if they would ever beat Kerry. Having disposed of a formidable Cavan 15 in the semi-final that year, they faced Kerry with confidence. Unfortunately, for the third year in a row, they found themselves on the wrong end of a scoreline that read: Kerry 2:7; Mayo 2:4.

However, back now to 1936. Victory over the Kingdom brought Mayo face to face with Leinster champions Laois in the final. It was a novel pairing. Laois were back boned by the Delaney clan — six of them, Tom, Tom (Senior), Bill, Chris, Mick, Jack — and Danny Douglas. Laois's credentials were very good. In the Leinster final Laois had a 3:3-to-0:8 victory over the previous year's defeated All-Ireland finalists, stylish Kildare. In the All-Ireland semi-final Laois defeated Cavan, the previous year's winners, by 2:6 to 1:5.

An epic final was in prospect. But it didn't materialise. On that fourth Sunday in September 1936, nothing went right for Laois. Unwisely, they played an injured Bill Delaney at midfield for the entire game. However, that of itself would hardly fully account for the Laois slump on the day. By contrast, Mayo were in devastating form and ran amok. They were rampant all over the field and romped home on a scoreline of 4:11 to 0:5 to take their first All-Ireland crown.

Mayo midfielder, Patsy Flannelly, had a field-day and played the proverbial 'blinder'. He was the outstanding man on the field — a field upon which, as a unit, the entire Mayo team displayed high levels of skill, speed, combination and accuracy. Defending the Railway goal they led by 2:5 to 0:2 at the break. The second half was more or less a carbon copy of the first, and that included the scoring, with Mayo adding 2:6 and their opponents taking only 3 points. They looked to be the perfect footballing combination. Their winning margin of 18 points was only once previously matched, by Kerry who outclassed Monaghan, in 1930.

The Mayo heroes of 1936 were:

Tom Bourke

Paddy Quinn, Jim McGowan, Purty Kelly

Tommy Regan, Seamus O'Malley (Captain), George Ormsby

Patsy Flannelly, Henry Kenny

Jackie Carney, Peter Laffey, Tommy Grier

Josie Munnelly, Paddy Moclair, Paddy Munnelly

The Mayo team of 1932

Josie Munnelly, at right corner-forward on the victorious 1936 team, had made his All-Ireland final début with Mayo's minor team in the 1933 final against Kerry. Twenty-four years later, at the age of 42, he was recalled by the Mayo selectors to man the same position in the All-Ireland junior football 'Home Final' against Cork, at Croke Park. Under the captaincy of Dr Mick Loftus, Warwickshire were defeated in the final and a proud Josie Munnelly collected his last All-Ireland medal.

In the League competition of 1934–35, Mayo emerged victorious from their first-round group. In subsequent games they firstly defeated Tipperary, in Clonmel, by 6:8 to 2:5; and then Fermanagh, in Castlebar, by 5:8 to 0:2 to take the title.

In the following season, 1935–36, Mayo captured the league for the third year in a row when they headed the league table with a total of 12 points from their eight games — hotly pursued by Dublin and Cavan with 10 points each.

The run of success continued for Mayo in the 1936–37 season when, in the deciding game at Croke Park on 11 April, Mayo beat Meath comfortably, by 5:4 to 1:8.

The National League has always been a test of endurance, stamina and consistency. When the 1937–38 competition got under way, the question being asked was could Mayo continue on the winning trail. The answer was given in the affirmative, in Castlebar on 3 July 1938, when the men of the west comprehensively defeated Wexford by 3:9 to 1:3 in the League final.

Earlier that year, on 24 April, Limerick had won a fifth successive National League hurling title. The odds that would have been given by any bookie, when the 1933–34 football and hurling leagues began, on the same two counties winning five successive titles, would surely have been astronomical.

But Mayo went one better than Limerick. They made it six in a row in football when they defeated Meath by 5:9 to 0:6, in Ballina, in the final of 1938–39. Mayo's remarkable record is very likely to stand for ever and a day.

Furthermore, they might well have bettered that record. However, for some reason they didn't participate in the 1939–40 competition. But they were back in action again in 1940-41 and took the title again by beating Dublin in the final at Croke Park, by 3:7 to 0:7. The competition was then suspended for the following four years because of wartime conditions

It must be said that, during the 1930s, the Mayo footballers were exceptional, despite the fact that they took only one All-Ireland crown. They won seven Connaught titles; toured America in 1932; made a major contribution to four memorable Railway Cup victories in 1934, 1936, 1937 and 1938 with Connaught. In those years Connaught defeated the cream of Leinster (1934), Ulster (1936) and Munster (1937 and 1938).

The 1934 and 1936 Connaught teams had eight Mayo men in their ranks. In 1937, ten Mayo men were selected and an eleventh came on as a substitute. In 1938, there were nine Mayo men and a tenth came on as a substitute.

It is well worth recalling the great names that represented Connaught in the 1938 Railway Cup football final and also the mighty men of Munster whom they defeated by 2:6 to 1:5 at Croke Park, on St Patrick's Day that year:

Connaught

Tom Bourke, Tommy Regan, Jim McGowan, Purty Kelly, Henry Kenny, Jackie Carney, Peter Laffey, Josie Munnelly, Paddy Moclair (all from Mayo); Mick Connaire, John Dunne, Charlie Connolly, Brendan Nestor, Mick Higgins (all from Galway); Patsy Flannelly of Mayo came on as a substitute.

Munster

Dan O'Keeffe, Johnny Walsh, Joe Keohane, Bill Casey, Bill Myers, Bill Dillon, T. Healy, Paddy Kennedy, John Joe Landers, Charlie O'Sullivan (all from Kerry); Tom Culhane of Limerick; C. Comerford, J. Burke (both from Clare); T. Cotter (from Cork); J. Slattery of Clare came on as a substitute.

In January 1961, Pádraig Puirséal selected his Football Finest (1930-1960). He put Tom Bourke of Mayo in goal, 'the greatest goalkeeper I ever saw in Croke Park was Tom Bourke of Mayo through the thirties'. He selected Paddy Moclair at right full forward. He gave consideration to three others, Purty Kelly at left full back, George Ormsby at left half-back and Henry Kenny at centre field.

Another great Mayo footballer of the 1930s was Gerald Courell, who won Railway Cup honours in 1934 with Connaught. He played with the cream of Ireland in the Tailteann Games of 1932. In the same year, when Mayo toured America, he was the star of the campaign, scoring 28 points from 5 games. His elusiveness, together with his speed, accuracy and his ground shot following a lovely dribble, set him apart as a brilliant half-forward. Football flowed freely in the genes of this Ballina native. His uncles, Frank, Joe and Bertie all played with Mayo in the early years of the twentieth century. Frank captained Mayo in 1916 when they lost the All-Ireland final to Wexford — the greatest footballing combination of that time — on the score of 2:4 to 1:2.

Mayo stars of the late 1940s and early 1950s

John Forde   *Peter Quinn*   *Padraig Carney*   *Tom Langan*

Peter Solan   *Eamonn Mongey*   *Tom Acton*

However, it wasn't just the Mayo senior footballers that brought pride and fame to Mayo in the 1930s. In 1933, the county junior team brought the first ever All-Ireland football title to Mayo. They beat Donegal in the home final by 2:15 to 2:2 and went on to beat London in the final by 3:7 to 2:4. Several members of that team, including Tommy Regan, Jackie Carney, Tommy Grier (who was captain), Peter Laffey and George Ormsby went on to form the nucleus of a great Mayo senior team.

Two years later, in 1935, the county minor team made the breakthrough. With a classy performance they defeated the champions of the jubilee years, Tipperary, on the score of 1:6 to 1:1.

All of the successes recounted above reflect the health and wellbeing of Mayo football in the 1930s — it is a decade to be proud of.

THE ALL-IRELAND HURLING FINAL DRAWS

As I write, it is the Autumn of 2000. One hundred and thirteen All-Ireland hurling championships have been played. Only four have gone to a replay after ending in a draw. The 1891 final between Kerry (Ballyduff) and Wexford (Crossabeg) did end all square, but extra time was played.

The results of those four finals:

1908
Tipperary 2:5; Dublin 1:8

Tipperary 3:15; Dublin 1:5

1931
Cork 1:6; Kilkenny 1:6

Cork 2:5; Kilkenny 2:5

Cork 5:8; Kilkenny 3:4

1934
Limerick 2:7; Dublin 3:4

Limerick 5:2; Dublin 2:6

1959
Waterford 1:17; Kilkenny 5:5

Waterford 3:12; Kilkenny 1:10.

It is interesting to note that on each occasion the Munster champions won the replay.

Each of the four drawn hurling finals has its own story and these are told in the following pages.

1908

Tipperary v Dublin

The final of 1908 was played at Jones's Road, on 25 April 1909. On that occasion Tipperary were represented by the Thurles Blues and the Dublin team was Kickhams. The match ended level.

In the early part of the twentieth century, hurling was still in the age of the seventeen-a-side game (an era that lasted from 1892 to 1912 inclusive). Incidentally, 1908 was the only draw that took place during that line-out format.

Also, in those days, the scoring area was larger than at present. A goal was scored between the soccer-like posts and points were scored within the sideposts, without any height restrictions (see Figure 1 on page 135).

On the way to the final, Tipperary had easily beaten Waterford in the first round. They then met Cork (Blackrock), in Fermoy, where the usual Titanic struggle ensued. The score was level at half-time with the teams on 1:4 each. Tipperary finally snatched victory with a late second-half goal. The final score was 2:11 to 3:7 in a match that was easily the best game of the 1908 championship.

The early years of the GAA championships were rarely free of controversy — objections, counter-objections, walk-overs, walk-offs, unfinished games and venue disputes all played their part. The Association was in its infancy and there were many growing pains. In 1908, Tipperary got a walk-over from Kerry in the Munster final and later on, another walk-over from Glasgow Irish.

The situation wasn't much different in Leinster that year, with Dublin getting a walk-over from Kilkenny. Tom Ryall in his book, *Kilkenny — The GAA Story 1884–1984* (The Kilkenny People, 1984), outlined the background of this as follows:

> *Kilkenny lost their first match in the 1908 championship to Wexford. It was played in Jones's Road. Wexford led at half-time by 1:6 to 0:5 and just held on in a great*

finish to triumph by 1 point, 1:8 to 0:10. The game had a sequel. Kilkenny objected to Wexford on the grounds that Sim Donohoe, who played in the junior football championship game against Kilkenny, which was the curtain-raiser to the senior game, had been sent to the line. They claimed he was not eligible for the hurling game.

Kilkenny wanted the game replayed but the Leinster Council Chairman, Dan McCarthy (Dublin), would not entertain the idea. He ruled Wexford out of the Championship. The Noresiders did not contest the Leinster final against Dublin . They had supplied 15 of the Leinster team that won the Railway Shield and felt they should be allowed to keep the shield.

The Leinster Council wanted to play-off a competition for the shield among the counties who had supplied players in Leinster wins. Kilkenny would not agree and when they failed to line-out against Dublin in the Leinster final, Dan McCarthy ruled them out of the championship and suspended them for six months.'

An appeal to Central Council resulted in Kilkenny being reinstated. At a subsequent meeting of the Leinster Council, custody of the shield was also granted to Kilkenny by an 8-to-6 majority.

A precedent had previously been set in Munster where the Munster Council had handed over the football shield to Kerry, as most of the winning team were from that county.

The Railway Shield was an inter-provincial competition and the first to win it twice in a row, or three times in all, retained the trophy. Leinster's win, on 19 July 1908, gave them two in a row. They defeated Munster by 14 points to 2:5 before 15,000 spectators, in Kilkenny.

The replay of the 1908 All-Ireland final took place in Athy, on 27 June 1909. After the drawn game it proved to be a big disappointment and an anti-climax. The game, refereed by Tom Irwin, Secretary of Cork County Board, ended 3:15 to 1:5 in Tipperary's favour. It was their eighth title.

They were captained by the renowned Tom Semple who was famed and revered, not only in his native Tipperary, but throughout the hurling world. Tom had said that the Athy sod was one of the best he had hurled on.

What is your fear boys when Semple is with you,
The gallant old captain who leads in the fray ...

Two years earlier he had led Tipperary (Thurles Blues) to All-Ireland honours in the 1906 final, played in Kilkenny, on 27 October 1907, against Dublin (Faughs). He won his first of three All-Ireland medals in 1900 and also led his club to six county title wins. He died in 1943 and, a quarter of a century later, the magnificent GAA grounds in Thurles were named in his honour. Other great names on the Tipperary team were Paddy Brolan, Hugh Shelly, and James 'The Hawk' O'Brien who played in goal.

Dublin also had names of renown. Jack Grace, of the famous Grace family of Tullaroan, was captain that year. He won All-Ireland football medals with Dublin in 1901, 1902, 1906, 1907, 1908 and was also captain of the team in 1906 and 1907. His brother, Pierce, who also won football medals in 1906 and 1907, was back with his native Kilkenny for the hurling successes of 1911, 1912 and 1913.

The Dublin goalkeeper was Andy Fitzgerald of Faughs. Despite many enquiries, I have failed to establish if he was one and the same person as Andy Fitzgerald, of goalkeeping fame, who minded the net for Cork in the All-Ireland final of 1912.

Tipperary's triumphant team was:

Tom Semple, Tom Kerwick, Jack Mockler, James 'Hawk' O'Brien,
Hugh Shelly, T. Carew, Jack Mooney, Tom Kenna,
Paddy Burke, Paddy Brolan, Joe McLoughney (Thurles),
Jim Burke (Two Mile Borris), Tim Gleeson, Mick Dwyer, (Holycross),
Jim and Pat Fitzgerald (New Bermingham), Martin O'Brien.

1931

Cork v Kilkenny

When referee Willie Walsh, of Waterford, blew the final whistle on the afternoon of Sunday, 1 November 1931, it signalled the end of an epic hurling marathon that had elevated the game of hurling onto a new plane.

It was also in 1931 that the name 'Cumann Lúthchleas Gael' was first used and that a score effected directly from a sideline puck was legalised.

Three hours of great hurling ended with Cork taking the MacCarthy Cup, but the honour of enriching our ancient game of hurling was shared equally by Kilkenny.

A total of 91,519 spectators saw the three games — games that saw fit hardy men pitted against each other, no quarter anywhere ('If you didn't get rid of the ball in my day, you got a flake of a man and the ball was flaked away from you' — Eudi Coughlan). There was drama, excitement, near misses, fierce man-to-man combat, passages of fast, superb hurling, with no time to settle on the ball (so fast was the action in the first replay that Dinny Barry Murphy of Cork said that, for a while, he was a little confused and added that it was no place for handymen), classical touches, great scores and disallowed scores also featured strongly throughout the play. It was one of the epics of hurling history — the stuff of folklore.

However, even epics have a downside. Some paid a heavy price. Dick Morrissey, of Kilkenny, was seriously injured in the first game and never hurled again. Paddy Larkin, of Kilkenny, broke his collar-bone in the second game and missed the replay. Lory Meagher, of Kilkenny, had ribs broken in the second game and was sorely missed in the third meeting.

Cork fielded the same team in all three games. In the replays, George Garrett came on to replace an injured player and performed brilliantly — he was one of hurling's great defenders, according to John Mackey.

Over the total of 180 minutes of the three games, every man became a hero. Spectators had much to reflect on. There was the Kilkenny captain, Lory Meagher — majestic — inspiring his men as he roamed the field, stealing a score from far out, sending in a beautifully placed ball, always marshalling his forces. His point from 90 yards was a gem.

Equally brilliant was Cork's captain, Eudi Coughlan, one of hurling's greatest wing forwards. He capped a supreme performance with a point from an awkward angle while on his knees. There was steel in Eudi. It is said that he gave his greatest ever display in the second replay of the 1931 All-Ireland final.

Dan Dunne, the Kilkenny corner forward, who marked 'Fox' Collins in all three matches, was the only man on the field to find the net in each game. He, together with Mattie Power, were Kilkenny's top forwards.

Cork's path to the final was as follows:

v Clare   *3:4 to 1:6*

v Tipperary   *3:5 to 2:3*

v Waterford   *1:9 to 4:0*

v Waterford   *5:4 to 1:2.*

Eudi Coughlan

The game against Tipperary was played before a capacity crowd at Thurles; thousands had to be turned away.

It was a testing campaign and if any of the games could be described as 'easy', it was the replay against Waterford.

Kilkenny played the following matches on their way to the final:

v Wexford   *8:8 to 1:1, in New Ross*

v Meath   *5:9 to 1:2, at Nowlan Park*

v Laois   *4:7 to 4:2, at Nowlan Park*

v Galway   *7:2 to 3:1, at Croke Park.*

Lory Meagher

Apart from the Laois game, it was an easy passage for Kilkenny. Indeed, when Laois scored four goals in the second half, to take the lead entering the last quarter, a surprise victory looked very possible. However, Kilkenny recovered to take the Leinster title.

Sean Robins, of Offaly, was the referee for the first two games. Kilkenny were seeking their ninth title and hadn't won a final since 1922. Cork were in search of their eleventh crown and, in doing so, were hoping to equal Tipperary's tally. Cork had the edge over Kilkenny in experience, having won All-Ireland titles in 1926, 1928 and 1929 — they had failed in the final of 1927, against Dublin.

The first game ended with scores of 1:6 each, after Cork had led 1:3 to 0:2, at half-time. The replay ended in a draw with the teams on 2:5 apiece — just seven scores each. Again, Cork had been leading at half-time, this time by 2:4 to 1:3. Indeed, in the second half of the second game, Cork got only one point, an equaliser — from Paddy Delea —

that was worth a King's Ransom, as Jim Hurley would have said. It was an era when scores were hard to come by. Frees were hard to come by too, as evidenced by the paucity of points. It was a case of first-timing the sliotar. It was man-to-man marking that called for courage, stamina, grit and grim resolve. Backs didn't stand on ceremony. There was no room for fancy stuff. A hand in the air was suicide — the idea of protecting it was a fairy-tale notion.

After the replay, officials wanted extra time played but Eudi Coughlan rejected it. He knew Kilkenny were younger. As far as he was concerned they would meet a third time.

At a Central Council meeting, it was suggested that both counties be declared joint champions but the motion was defeated.

Thus the contest went to a second replay, a third meeting and the making of a piece of GAA history. The clock ticked towards half-time and with two minutes to go, despite the loss of Lory and others, the scores were level: Cork 0:5; Kilkenny 1:2. Then Cork struck with two goals via 'Gah' Aherne and Paddy Delea. Their supporters sensed victory and at the interval shouted, 'Glory to old Rockies, no draw this time'. 'The Rockies', of course, were Blackrock who had eight players on the Cork team — nine if you were to count George Garrett.

After that, the pressure told on Kilkenny and, despite coming within a point of Cork in the second half, they were forced to give way to a better team on the day. Cork won by 5:8 to 3:4. At one stage, in the second half, a Kilkenny player went down injured and the story is told of a girl whose emotions overflowed into tears. She, and others, begged Lory with chants of 'Lory, Lory, Lory', to urge him respond to the need of his county; but he couldn't.

As a gesture of appreciation of the legendary performances displayed by Cork and Kilkenny, the Central Council presented wristlet watches to the members of both teams.

In Cork, each team member was presented with a miniature gold hurley — a most appropriate way to end a Cork golden era. Eudi Coughlan proudly showed me his award when I interviewed him, in 1981, for my book *Giants of the Ash* (Wolfhound Press, 1991). He also showed me the three sliotars used in those games on each of which was inscribed the score of the game. Then he told me that it was his last championship game for Cork. 'Cork took the selection from my club in 1932 so that finished my time for Cork. I never put on a red jersey for them again.'

The following were the heroes of 1931:

Cork

John Coughlan (Blackrock)

Morgan Madden (Redmonds), E. 'Marie' O'Connell (Blackrock)
Paddy 'Fox' Collins (Glen Rovers)

Dinny Barry Murphy (Éire Óg), Jim O'Regan (Éire Óg)
Tom Barry (Carrigtwohill)

Mick O'Connell (St Finbarrs), Jim Hurley (Blackrock)

Eudi Coughlan (Blackrock), Paddy 'Balty' Aherne (Blackrock)
Peter 'Hawker' O'Grady (Blackrock)

Paddy Delea (Blackrock), Willie Clancy (Mallow)
Michael 'Gah' Aherne (Blackrock).

George Garrett of Blackrock came on as a substitute in both replays, for Morgan Madden and Peter O'Grady respectively.

Kilkenny

Jim Dermody (Tullaroan)

Paddy Larkin (James Stephens), Peter O'Reilly (Dicksboro)
Billy Dalton(Carrickshock)

Tommy Carroll (Mooncoin), Paudge Byrne (Dicksboro)
Eddie Doyle (Mooncoin)

Lory Meagher (Tullaroan), Ned Byrne (Dicksboro)

Paddy Phelan (Tullaroan), Martin White (Tullaroan)
Dick Morrissey (Mooncoin)

Dan Dunne (Dicksboro), Mick Larkin (James Stephens)
Mattie Power (Garda, Dublin).

Day One: Jack Duggan, of Mooncoin, replaced the injured Dick
   Morrissey
Day Two: Jack Duggan retained his place.
   Paddy 'Skipper' Walsh, of Tullaroan, took the place of Martin White.
   Tommy Leahy, of Urlingford, came on as a substitute for Lory.
Day Three: Jack Duggan, Paddy 'Skipper Walsh and Tommy Leahy all
   retained their places.
   Jerry Leahy of Urlingford, and Dinny Treacy, lined out in place of
   Paddy Larkin and Bill Dalton, who were both injured.

1934

Limerick v Dublin

In 1934, the GAA celebrated its jubilee year marking the anniversary of
its foundation. A special set of medals was struck to commemorate the
occasion and inscribed: 'Bliain an Iúbaile 1934'. There was, therefore,
an added incentive for all the hurling counties to make an extra special
effort. They all wanted to be crowned champions.

In Leinster, Kilkenny — reigning All-Ireland champions — started
their campaign with a rather fortunate two-point win over Laois, at
Nowlan Park. The following weekend they departed to the US on a six-
week tour. On their return, they faced Dublin in the Leinster final, at
Portlaoise. With five minutes to go Kilkenny were down 8 points. They
then put in one of their sensational finishes and scored 3 goals that
were followed by an equalising point from Dublin. The match finished
on the score, Dublin 2:8; Kilkenny 4:2.

The replay was played at the same venue. At half-time, Dublin led
by 3:3 to nil, and at the final whistle were Leinster champions on the
score of 3:5 to 2:2 — they were, of course, also through to the All-
Ireland final.

In Munster, Limerick were the provincial title-holders and had been
All-Ireland finalists of the previous year. In the spring of 1934, they
captured their first National League title with a three-point win over
Dublin. In that game John Mackey was Man-of-the-Match and without
him, Limerick would more than likely have lost. Limerick then set their
eyes firmly on the jubilee medals.

There were no easy games (score lines can be deceptive) along Limerick's path to the All-Ireland final, which was as follows:

v Clare   *6:4 to 3:2, at Limerick Gaelic Grounds*

v Cork   *3:4 to 2:2, at Thurles*

v Waterford *4:8 to 2:5, at Cork*

v Galway   *4:4 to 2:4, at Roscrea.*

No collective training was done for the first of Limerick's games. A panel of twenty-two players had been selected and told to get themselves match-fit. For the game against Cork, they spent ten evenings under the watchful eye of Dinny Lanigan. It was only when the players assembled, in Thurles, that the team selection was announced. Limerick got off to a flying start with two goals from their youthful newcomer, Jackie O'Connell, who was being marked by no less a defender than George Garrett. Five minutes into the second half, Cork drew level with a goal from Micka Brennan. This brought the score to 2:2 apiece and it stayed that way for a further twenty minutes as the tide of battle ebbed and flowed with neither team's defence yielding an inch.

Then it happened — all in the space of five minutes. A Mick Mackey solo run, from midfield to the 40-yard line, saw a pass to Dave Clohessy flashed to the net. The deadlock was broken. Mick got possession again and sent over a point. Within a minute, his brother, John, scored a great point from far out. Referee Tommy Daly, of Clare, blew full time and the score read: Limerick 3:4; Cork 2:2 — victory, but oh, so close!

Victory over Waterford — only clinched in the last quarter — saw Limerick retain their provincial crown. Next, it was Galway that barred the way to Croke Park but they were defeated after a tough, most uncompromising, and at times, far too robust encounter.

In 1934, Dublin and Limerick met in an All-Ireland hurling final for the second time. On the first occasion, in the final of 1921, played on 4 March 1923, a powerful Limerick team had won by 8:5 to 3:2. Two players — Bob McConkey and Garret Howard — had been on the victorious Limerick team of 1921. However, this time it would be much harder for them.

Dublin's strength lay in their very high level of physical fitness. Many of them were Garda and Army men. Indeed, very few were natives of Dublin. It was a combination of men from Cork, Tipperary, Waterford, Laois and Westmeath. They were excellent hurlers. It's a measure of their brilliance to say that they were in Kilkenny's class.

An attendance of almost 35,000 spectators turned up for the final and they witnessed a battle royal. Great men marked great men. In a game where hurling skills and fierce physical exchanges were interwoven and entwined, there was no room for any flaws of the spirit. The closeness of the game is reflected in the half-time score of 1:5 to 2:1, in Limerick's favour.

Scores continued to be at a premium in the second half. Up to the final minutes Limerick were a goal to the good, but Dinny O'Neill, for Dublin, snatched the equaliser.

The replay was fixed for Sunday, 30 September.

In preparation for this game, Limerick had the benefit of the training guidance of Jim Barry, of Cork. He placed emphasis on ground hurling, conscious now of what was required if Dublin were to be overcome. Then came the shock of shocks — brilliant custodian Paddy Scanlon was sidelined with a blood-poisoned finger. Limerick then turned to former county and Munster goalkeeper, Tommy Shinny, to replace Paddy in goal.

They travelled to Dublin by early train on Saturday morning and spent the afternoon touring the beauty spots of Wicklow, by coach.

The next day they were at Croke Park for the business of the 1934 All-Ireland final. Referee Stephen Jordan, of Galway, got the game under way. Limerick defended the Canal end and had the advantage of a slight breeze. The trend of play followed the pattern of the drawn game — close, hard, fast and physical hurling. The teams were level at half-time, Dublin 0:3; Limerick 1:0. With two minutes remaining, and the teams still level, Mick Mackey whipped-over a point for the lead. Then, in the space of the 90 seconds remaining, Jackie O'Connell shot a point and Dave Clohessy found the net. The full time score — Limerick 5:2; Dublin 2:6. Thus Limerick became All-Ireland champions in the jubilee year of 1934 and became proud owners of the anniversary medals.

In both games Limerick's leading scorer was Dave Clohessy who ran up a personal tally of 6:2. Dublin's top scorer was Dinny O'Neill, who took a total of 4:2.

Reporting on the game in the *Cork Weekly Examiner*, 'Carbery' had this to say:

Some will say that last Sunday's replay was slightly behind the 1931 Cork–Kilkenny game in brilliant quality, but I must write here and now that in the 35 hurling finals I have seen, never a one approached last Sunday's in uniform thrill, in speed, in magnificent ground play, where every man of the 30 was fit and, I might say, inspired by the momentous issue involved. Never have I seen fitter men and rarely have hurling lovers watched a game of such superb quality.

Every man burst to his sprints on the ball like Olympic runners. Tackling was staggering in its intensity. A visitor from America seated in the stand behind me proffered the opinion that he'd like to play hurling in a wire cage. Yet, so perfectly controlled was each man's swing of ash that accidents were few and minor.

What struck me most about this game, as compared with the great finals of the past, was the power and quality of the ground hurling. Towards the end Limerick were finishing at a rare pace, yet up to their hips stood the staunch Dublin men. It was a finish for the Gods ... so did this consistent Garryowen team recover the championship after 13 years. Never were trophies more nobly won. Limerick City and County are justly proud of their splendid team.

Another press report read:

The pace was terrific, the marking, perhaps, the closest ever seen. The game was one sweep of clenched courage. It was the epic close of the season's classics. Great men won and great men lost. Their names shall be remembered for ever.

In the Hogan Stand, Archbishop Harty, Patron of the Association — a native of Limerick himself — presented the MacCarthy Cup to Timmy Ryan, the captain of the victorious Limerick team, amid enthusiastic scenes of joy and jubilation. Then the Boherbuoy Band, to the strains of 'Garryowen', led the way in triumph to Barry's Hotel — and further celebrations.

Limerick

Tom Shinny (Fedamore)

Ned Cregan (Newcastle West), Tom McCarthy (Fedamore)
Mick Kennedy (Young Irelands)

Mickey Cross (Claughaun), Paddy Clohessy (Fedamore)
Garret Howard (Portroe)

Timmy Ryan (Ahane), Mick Ryan (Murroe)

John Mackey (Ahane), Mick Mackey (Ahane), Jim Roche (Croom)

Jackie O'Connell (Croom), Dave Clohessy (Fedamore)
Jimmy Close (Ahane)

Paddy Scanlon and Bob McConkey played in the drawn game.
Seven of the Limerick team were on the Munster Railway Cup team
that defeated Leinster with seven of the Dublin team — 3:4 to 3:0 —
on St Patrick's Day, 1935. Paddy Scanlon, Tom McCarthy, Paddy
Clohessy, Timmy Ryan, Mick Mackey, John Mackey and Mick Kennedy.

The Limerick Team of 1934

1959

Waterford v Kilkenny

With a minute left in the 1959 All-Ireland final, the score read: Kilkenny 5:5; Waterford 0:17. Then, Seamus Power snatched a reprieve from the jaws of defeat. Following a solo run, Seamus took a shot that deflected off the hurley of full back Jim Walsh, and past his namesake Ollie in goal. As everyone among the crowd of 73,707 looked forward to a repeat of what had been a superb final, the energetic Seamus Power grabbed the sliotar from the puck out and everyone held their breath as his shot for the winning point went ever-so-narrowly wide. Eagerly, we looked forward to the replay.

With Antrim not participating in the senior championship, and Galway having entered the championship in Munster there would be no All-Ireland semi-final in 1959. The winners of the Munster and Leinster championships would meet in the All-Ireland final and, in the event, it turned out to be a repeat of 1957 when Waterford met Kilkenny.

The teams took the following routes to the 1959 All-Ireland final:

Waterford

v Galway	7:11 to 0:8,	in Limerick
v Tipperary	9: 3 to 3:4,	in Cork
v Cork	3: 9 to 2:9,	in Thurles.

In the game against Tipperary, Waterford were facing the reigning All-Ireland champions. Tipperary were favourites after the 4:12-to-1:5 trouncing they had given Waterford in the Munster final the previous year. Tipperary, who won the toss and opted to play against the wind, caught a tartar in Waterford. The Waterford forwards mesmerised the Tipperary defence and ran up a half-time lead of over 8 goals against the reigning champions.

Against Cork, at Thurles, Joe Harney had the better of Ring, and Grimes was superb. Waterford won a thrilling game in a close contest and looked very formidable.

Kilkenny

v *Laois*   *8:10 to 2: 4, in Birr*

v *Dublin*   *2: 9 to 1:11, at Croke Park.*

If the game against Laois turned out to be practice stuff, the Leinster final, against Dublin, was almost Kilkenny's undoing — indeed, it should have been. Time-added-on was being played when Sean Clohessy finished a sideline cut to the net to put Kilkenny 1 point ahead. The puck out from that score brought with it the final whistle. It was, what the late Micheál O'Hehir would have described as, an 'act of grand larceny', and it left Dublin players and fans bewildered and wondering, as they made their way home.

Gerry Fitzgerald, of Limerick, got the final under way on 6 September. It was a cracker. Waterford set the pace, led by their classy captain, Frankie Walsh. However, every time they forged ahead and looked the better team, they were pulled back by Kilkenny, who were captained by the stylish Sean Clohessy. The final score of Kilkenny 5:5; Waterford 1:17, tells its own story. Supremacy in lots of positions for Waterford; Kilkenny getting through for killer-punch goals — Tommy O'Connell their teenage corner forward got three. Ollie Walsh's performance in goal warranted superlatives — the last-minute deflection denied him a clean slate. The score line mightn't suggest it, but Ollie's opposite number, Ned Power, also had a brilliant game. For a change it was Waterford who did a 'Kilkenny' on the match, by saving the day, when all seemed lost.

So on to the replay on 4 October and expectations of more thrills.

'Oh for the clash of the ash so sweet
The flying ball and the hurlers fleet'

Carbery

Trainer John Keane — hurling hero of many a hectic hour — prepared Waterford well for the replay, both physically and mentally.

On 4 October, Gerry Fitzgerald, again, got the game under way — this time before an increased attendance of 77,285 people — they weren't disappointed; what a final it was.

Kilkenny had the better of the first-quarter exchanges, despite playing against a lively breeze; but by half-time Waterford had forged ahead 3:5 to 1:8. Waterford upped the momentum in the second half. They concentrated on ground hurling and tackled fearlessly. They whipped the sliotar hither and yon and opened the way for scores. They had learned from the drawn game. The full back line didn't crowd the goalkeeper, Ned Power, and his performance rivalled that of Ollie's. If Sean Clohessy was brilliant for Kilkenny, Waterford's Frankie Walsh was certainly Man-of-the-Match.

However, it was a day when every Waterford man was a hero. They had a strong midfield partnership in Seamus Power and Phil Grimes. Corner back Joe Harney saw to it that Tommy O'Connell got no score this time. The unorthodox and indestructible Tom Cheasty, from his centre forward position, finished with a personal score tally of 2:2,— joint top scorer of the day with Frankie Walsh, who took 8 points. The silver-haired Johnny Kiely played his usual intelligent hurling. Once the Waterford defence steadied, after the first quarter, the team clicked as a unit. They were most worthy winners of their second title, on the score 3:12 to 1:10.

The MacCarthy Cup returned in triumph to Waterford after a lapse of eleven years; and proudly did they bear it, for among the spoils of victory were the colours they had lowered — the red and white, the blue and gold, the black and amber — of the 'Big Three': Cork, Tipperary and Kilkenny.

The Waterford team of 1959

Waterford's heroes lined-out as follows:

Ned Power (Tallow)

Joe Harney (Ballydurn), Austin Flynn (Abbeyside)
John Barron (De la Salle)

Mick Lacey (Cappoquin), Martin Óg Morrissey (Mount Sion)
Jackie Condon (Erin's Own)

Seamus Power (Mount Sion), Phil Grimes (Mount Sion)

Mick Flannelly (Mount Sion),Tom Cheasty (Ballyduff)
Frankie Walsh (captain) (Mount Sion)

Larry Guinan (Mount Sion), Tom Cunningham (Dungarvan)
John Kiely (Éire Óg)

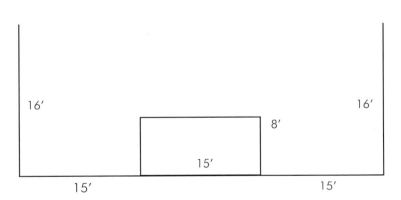

Figure 1 — *The Scoring Area 1908*

TIPPERARY'S TRIPLE HURLING SUCCESS

When I think of Matt the Thrasher's strength
And Nora Leahy's grace,
I love you Tipperary though
I never saw your face.

It is most unlikely that a betting man, studying form, would have come up with a treble of victories — in senior, junior and minor hurling — for Tipperary in the All-Ireland championships of 1930. (At that time, the grading system consisted of only these three categories).

At senior level, anyone placing a bet in the championship that year would very likely have plumped for Cork — they had won four titles in a row in Munster, from 1926 to 1929 inclusive. Also, during that time, they had taken three All-Ireland titles, failing only against Dublin in 1927. In addition, they had won the Leagues of 1925–26 and 1929–30. Thus in 1930, they seemed to be the team most on form with a very strong panel of players and no apparent weaknesses.

The thirteenth championship at junior level was competed for in 1930 and, statistically, Tipperary would have been the best bet. They had won two of their four titles in 1924 and 1926 and had lost the final by only 2 points to Kilkenny in 1928.

The minor championship was a relatively new innovation which had begun in 1928. Cork and Waterford took the first two titles, defeating Dublin and Meath respectively. The competition was very much a lottery and this was compounded by the fact that players were not always of the correct 'minor' age. The requirement that team members had to be under 18 years of age on 1 January wasn't being adhered to in some quarters.

Tipperary's Senior Victory

The 1930 Munster senior hurling semi-final, between Waterford and Tipperary, was played in Dungarvan before an attendance of about 10,000 spectators. Waterford had beaten Limerick in a thrill-packed encounter, before a capacity crowd that paid total gate receipts of £360, in Waterford. They faced Tipperary with high hopes. 'Ach ní mar síltear bítear'. Tipperary were leading Waterford by 2:5 to 0:1 when an altercation occurred between the players. It led to the game being abandoned and referee, Seán Óg Murphy of Cork, subsequently awarded the game to Tipperary.

The other semi-final was played in Limerick where Clare caused the shock of the year by defeating the All-Ireland champions, Cork, on the score of 6:6 to 5:6. Clare's victory made them the favourites in the Munster final against Tipperary who hadn't won a title since 1925.

However, Tipperary, despite having a lighter team than Clare, were quietly confident. In goal they had Tommy O'Meara, brother of John 'Skinny' O'Meara (who had enjoyed previous fame). Tommy hated forwards going in on top of him and the Tipperary backs were instructed to keep the Clare forwards out of the goal area. This they did, and consequently Tommy had an inspired hour. In the forward line Tipperary had two of Ireland's greatest forwards — Martin Kennedy and Phil Cahill. The team was captained by veteran John Joe Callinan who had played for Dublin when they won the All-Ireland title, in 1920. However, and perhaps most importantly of all, Tipperary had been trained by Tom Semple — that wily warrior of old — who had won three All-Ireland medals in the first decade of the twentieth century.

Great hurling, played at speed, was the feature of the first half of the Munster final which was played at Cork Athletic Grounds. Tipperary, having played with the wind, led by only 1 point at the break. Their prospects weren't looking good. Play resumed and, as sometimes happens, the game was won and lost in a sudden short burst of play. In a little over five minutes, Tipperary had found the net twice via Tommy Leahy and John Joe Callinan. These two goals put them 7 points ahead and, in the end, they won the Munster title by 8 points. The game was refereed by Seán Óg Murphy of Cork and Frank Daly, the Lord Mayor of Cork, threw in the ball to start the match.

Tipperary, with Phil Purcell giving the most outstanding performance, easily overcame Galway, in Birr, in awful weather conditions. They then went on to meet Dublin in the All-Ireland final which was played on Sunday, 7 September 1930.

On that occasion, Dublin actually had five Tipperary men in their ranks: John Dwyer, Tom Quinlan, Tom Burke, Tom Teehan, Tom O'Meara; in addition a sixth, Mick Daniels, came on as a substitute. They were captained by the renowned Kilkennyman Jim 'Builder' Walsh. Dublin also had the services of the great Galway midfielder, Mick Gill, who won All-Ireland medals with his native Galway in 1923 and his adopted Dublin in 1924; and also in 1927, when he had the honour of being captain.

In the forward line they also had Kilkennyman Mattie Power, who was one of the greatest forwards the game has ever known.

Dublin then presented the last obstacle to Tipperary's eleventh All-Ireland crown. The Munster men were fortunate to be 1 point ahead at the interval. However, Johnny Leahy, hero of 100 battles in the Tipperary colours, had this to say to Carbery at the time:

'We were a point in front at half-time against Waterford, the same against Galway and Clare, and now the same against Dublin. 'Tis a good omen; the fireworks will come, and you'll see us galloping through.'

The prophecy was delivered. Typical Tipperary dash asserted itself in the second half. They switched into a higher gear and won by a total of 7 points. Tommy Treacy at midfield had a memorable performance:

'The work done at midfield by Treacy was grand
And the cheers for that hero came back from the stand.
'Twill live in our memory until we are dead
And the crimson stained bandage he wore round his head.'

The Tipperary team returned on Monday evening to an enthusiastic reception in Thurles where Dr Harty, Patron of the Association, addressed the happy gathering. On Sunday 12 October the victory was also marked when Cashel Gaels organised a victory dance to celebrate the senior hurling triumph.

Five of that victorious team — Tommy O'Meara, Phil Purcell, Tommy Treacy, Martin Kennedy and Phil Cahill — lined-out for Munster on the following St Patrick's Day when they defeated Leinster by 1:12 to 2:6 in the Railway Cup final of 1931.

Tipperary's Minor Victory

Jack Russell, of Thurles, led the Tipperary minors to victory over Cork in the Munster final; it was a good win: 4:3 to 3:0.

In the earlier rounds they had won:

v Kerry at Mallow — 7:1 to 4:2

v Waterford at Thurles — 4:0 to 2:1.

In the All-Ireland final they met Kilkenny who had devastated Down in the semi-final by 12:1 to 2:1. However, against Tipperary, the road to goal was more difficult for Kilkenny and their forwards squandered golden scoring opportunities. As a result, Tipperary had a somewhat lucky victory on the score of 4:1 to 2:1. The game was played on 28 September 1930 as a curtain-raiser to the All-Ireland football final between Kerry and Monaghan.

Tipperary's Junior Victory

The Tipperary junior team, under the mentorship of the renowned Johnny Leahy and captained by Patrick Harty of Borrisoleigh, had the following successful campaign in Munster, in 1930:

v Kerry in Tralee — 4:5 to 0:5

v Limerick in Clonmel — 4:7 to 4:7; replay — 5:4 to 2:5

v Clare in Thurles — 7:4 to 1:2.

It will be of interest to readers to learn that Mick Mackey was a member of the Limerick team in the above match.

Tipperary beat London easily in the All-Ireland semi-final, at Croke Park, before only a handful of spectators. They then faced Kilkenny, who had been held to a draw by Antrim in the semi-final, in Belfast, and had been hard-pressed to win the replay which ended on the score of 4:1 to 1:4. As Tipperary's enthusiastic supporters headed for Waterford on 23 November the big question was whether they could defeat Kilkenny and do what no county had ever done — capture the three All-Ireland hurling crowns in the same year.

It was nip-and-tuck in the first quarter. There was little between the teams. At half-time Tipperary were wary, despite the fact that they were leading by 2:4 to 1:1. On resumption of play they piled on the pressure and finished in a blaze of glory with two late goals. Neutral fans, in a crowd of up to 10,000 people, were disappointed in a rather one-sided finish. However, on a final score of 6:8 to 3:2, Tipperary achieved what surely could only have been a dream at the beginning of the hurling season of 1930.

Ned Wade, later to play senior hurling with Tipperary and Dublin, achieved a personal double in 1930, having played on both the minor and junior winning teams.

Recalling the great successes of 1930, Sliabh Ruadh wrote as follows:

> *By winning the three All-Irelands for 1930 in hurling — senior, junior and minor — Tipperary achieved a unique distinction in GAA history. Reverend John Meagher, Chairman of the Tipperary County Board, offered a prize of £5 for the best poem on the subject and this was won by Tom Hickey of Fethard. There were several excellent attempts sent in, which have been published in neat booklet form by the* Tipperary Star. *I shall be pardoned for concluding my last chapter on the* History of the GAA for Twenty Years *by quoting a beautiful quatrain by Miss Hayes, of Cashel:*
>
> *'It's not a crown of diamonds,*
> *nor yet a crown of gold,*
> *But a treble crown of laurels*
> *That speaks of fame untold.'*

To date no county has had similar success.

Congratulations on the great achievement came from home and abroad. Father James B. Dollard (Sliav-na-Mon), writer, poet, nationalist, lover of all things Gaelic — especially hurling — sent the following message from Toronto:

> *Surely the homes of Tipperary will be happy this Christmas, having the hay saved, Cork and Clare "bet", Galway and Dublin in the shade, and dear old Slievenamon proudly gazing on prostrate Kilkenny. I always thought that the old mountain rejoices when Tipperary hurlers are triumphant and weeps when they are defeated — and why shouldn't it? Hurling and Slievenamon are the two most ancient survivals in Tipperary; they have been friends for thousands of years.*

In those lines I sense the lament of an exile — '*I bhfad ó mo dhaoine idir dhá thír*'.

Slievenamon seems to conjure up something magical and majestic for its exiles. A few years ago, Fr Sean Reid, a Carmelite priest, who celebrated his ninetieth birthday in February 2000, sent me a poem that he had written about this mystical mountain. A Kilkennyman, Fr Reid spent most of his life in the sacred ministry in the United States. He was Grand Marshal of the St Patrick's Day Parade in New York, in the 1960s, and is a scholar and a poet. The poem is titled 'Slievenamon' and I feel honoured to be able to publish it here.

Patrick Harty   *John Joe Callanan*   *Jack Russell*

Slievenamon

I saw sunrise this morning
As it shone upon
Distinct in the distance
The slopes of Slievenamon
It sometimes has headgear
Bonnet of white clouds
Today it is bareheaded
Standing aloof and proud.

I am in County Kilkenny
Slievenamon is far away
A vision on the horizon
Well-defined on clear day
Rain clouds as if by magic
At a word of command
Gone a disappearing act
At wave of magician's hand.

Next morning at sunrise
I look to the west
Back to us is given
Our own Mount Everest
Not our highest mountain
Easy is it to climb
Grassland to the summit
From there a view sublime.

O Slievenamon symmetrical
Alluring to the sight
Whenever you are visible
In the morning sunlight
You forecast the weather
What the day will bring
Will we see some sunshine
Or hear rain spattering.

When you wear a bonnet
A shower will we see
When you are invisible
Rain you guarantee
When you are bareheaded
Cloudless at awakening
Sunshine in the offing
That the news you bring.

O Slievenamon invisible
We know you are there
As you were for poets
Who with us still share
Visions of beguilement
As you they gazed upon
Songsters keep on singing
Of you sweet Sievenamon.

VICTORY AGAINST THE ODDS — OFFALY STYLE

1980

In 1969, Offaly appeared in their sixth Leinster hurling final — their first since 1928 — having defeated the reigning All-Ireland champions, Wexford, in the semi-final. They came within a whisker of beating a great and star-studded Kilkenny team in the provincial final. The match ended 3:9 to 0:16 points, and Kilkenny went on to take the All-Ireland crown with a victory over Cork. It was an ageing Offaly team who played Kilkenny: they had been attempting to break through since the mid-sixties. Now, however, they had served warning that hurling in Offaly had real potential. It took a dozen years to blossom.

Leinster final day 1980: Kilkenny, All-Ireland title holders versus a Cinderella team — Offaly. At the time, the magazine *Sports World* carried a front-page heading: 'Easy for Kilkenny'; hurling fans thought the same. Only 9,613 people turned up for the game, the smallest attendance of modern times for a provincial final and a mere handful in the vast expanses of Croke Park. However, those who came witnessed a piece of hurling history. Offaly, coached both physically and mentally by Kilkennyman Dermot Healy, one of hurling's shrewdest mentors, carried the day in a nail-biting encounter. There was just one point in it — 3:17 to 5:10. It was a first-ever Leinster crown for the county and the victory was to prove the harbinger of great days in Offaly hurling over the next two decades.

1981

In 1981, Offaly captured their second Leinster hurling title with a 2-point win over Wexford — 3:12 to 2:13. They had already put Laois to the sword with a dramatic last-minute point from a 90-yard free by Paddy Kirwan in a high-scoring, rip-roaring game. These wins paved the way for an All-Ireland showdown against Galway in the final on the first Sunday in September 1981. It was a novel pairing — Offaly's first final, Galway's thirteenth — and it drew a crowd of 71,384 spectators, the largest attendance since 1963.

The pundits favoured Galway; after all, they were the reigning All-Ireland champions at the time. A glance at their line-out showed that the team was endowed with a wealth of talent and experience — few, if any, wondered about it being their thirteenth final. Neither did anyone dwell closely on the fact that, in the 1980 All-Ireland semi-final, Galway — although the better team on the day — had been fortunate to survive against Offaly.

Referee Frank Murphy, of Cork, got the 1981 final under way on a day of good weather conditions. In the first half, Galway looked classy, assured and rather casual. On the other hand Offaly — solid, tenacious and disciplined — concentrated on the basics of the game. Pat Delaney at the Offaly centre half-back position epitomised all of that, and inspired his colleagues with some great long-range points.

An interesting first half ended with Galway — who were rather unfortunate to have had a goal disallowed — leading by 0:13 to 1:4. There were those in the crowd who felt Galway would open the floodgates in the second half and win pulling up. No one, however, could have envisaged that a point in the fourth minute of the second half, which would give Galway a 7-point lead, would be their second-last score of the match.

All the drama of the occasion was packed into the closing ten minutes. By that stage, the scoreboard read: Galway 0:15; Offaly 1:9. Galway had been very wasteful but it looked as if they would hold out. The passage of time can play tricks with the mind but, if my memory serves me right, it was after this that Noel Lane tore menacingly through the Offaly defence. He sent a sizzler for the top right-hand

corner of the net. It would have beaten many a goalkeeper but the
ever-alert Damien Martin brought off a super reflex save. Looking
back with the benefit of hindsight one cannot help feeling that, if Noel
had taken a point and stretched the Galway lead to four points, Galway
might have prevailed.

Five minutes to go. An Offaly point cuts the lead to 2 points.
Tension mounts. The referee's watch ticks on. Now three minutes
remain. Johnny Flaherty is in possession following an Offaly attack
involving Joachim Kelly, Pat Delaney and Brendan Bermingham. Out
of nothing, Will-o'the-Wisp Johnny conjures up a goal from a palmed
effort over his shoulder. Pandemonium. Offaly one point ahead.
Galway are visibly in shock. Time ticks on. Offaly add two more points
via Danny Owens and Padraic Horan. A last desperate effort by
Galway to snatch a draw goes wide of the upright. Frank Murphy
blows full time. The faithful county proudly takes possession of the
Liam MacCarthy Cup.

1982

The year 1982 would have roughly marked the centre of what was
probably the greatest dozen years in Kerry football. It began with a
famous win in 1975 over a well-fancied Dublin team. It ended in 1986
when Tyrone were defeated in the All-Ireland final. In that era Kerry
won eight All-Ireland crowns and three National League titles. The
players won an abundance of All-Star awards. The team, an immensely
talented one, was the talk of the land.

Meanwhile, within that era, Offaly, one of the great dual counties of
modern times, were assembling an effective football combination. The
following are some key results:

Leinster Finals

1979: v Dublin — lost 1:8 to 0:9

1980: v Dublin — won 1:10 to 1.8

1981: v Laois — won 1:18 to 3:9

1982: v Dublin — won 1:16 to 1:7

Post Leinster Finals

1980 A/I semi-final: v Kerry — lost 4:15 to 4:10

1981 A/I final: v Kerry — lost 1:12 to 0:8

1982 A/I semi-final: v Galway won 1:12 to 1:11.

During the years in question, Offaly were playing quality football and they had an outstanding goalkeeper in Martin Furlong — well-known for his penalty saves. However, the brilliance of Kerry overshadowed everything in those days. The Offaly performances weren't being deeply analysed. All the better for Offaly, therefore, when they faced Kerry in the 1982 All-Ireland final. Naturally, Kerry were the universal favourites. Victory would give them an unprecedented five-in-a-row All-Ireland title achievement. It would create a new record in the annals of the GAA and would lift Kerry, and in particular the players directly linked to the achievement, on to a new plateau of fame and immortality.

However, those who believed in portents would have warned Kerry to be very cautious, to convert every opportunity and to bear in mind that when Caesar told the soothsayer that the Ides of March had come, he was quietly reminded that they had not yet gone.

And the portent? Yes, it was there alright. In the years 1971, 1972, 1973, 1974 and 1977 Kerry won the National League title and in each of those years they failed in the All-Ireland campaign. As against that, when they won the All-Ireland titles of 1975, 1978, 1979, 1980 and 1981, they were unsuccessful in the League.

Now, in 1982, they were facing Offaly in the All-Ireland final with the 1982 League cup on the sideboard — but no one said to the Kerry team: 'Beware the League Cup'.

It was a fine All-Ireland final between two great football teams. Midway through the second half Kerry, leading by 1 point, were awarded a penalty and Mikey Sheehy was entrusted with the kick. There was no warning for Mikey: 'Beware the League Cup'; 'Beware Martin Furlong facing penalties' — Martin Furlong saved the penalty.

Still, with time running out, Kerry were three points up — and looking good for the five-in-a-row All-Ireland record. Then a 21-yard free to Offaly in front of the goal was pointed and it cut the Kerry lead to only 2 points. However, time was ominously ticking away for Offaly — perhaps about 2 minutes to go.

Offaly won a free around midfield. You'd swear by the casual and nonchalant way they set about taking it that they were in the lead and just killing time. Without any fuss or apparent urgency, Mick Fitzgerald took a short free to Richie Connor who parted to full back Liam O'Connor, who had advanced up-field in support. He let fly a high one from the right wing towards the left of the Kerry goal — down, down, down it came. Seamus Darby, who had come in as a substitute, soared high and caught cleanly. The Kerry cover was thin. Seamus turned and his shot shook the rigging; he danced a jig. The scoreboard read: Offaly 1:15; Kerry 0:17. It was the kind of score that Micheál O'Hehir used to describe as an act of grand larceny. Offaly were back from the grave. Kerry had an opportunity to secure a draw but wasted it. The final whistle blew. No one had said: 'Kerry beware'.

1994

There is, in the Offaly psyche, a resilience, a composure, an equanimity that enables its sportsmen to withstand situations where the odds are heavily stacked against them. When all seems lost they seem to emerge with a formula that produces dramatic and, on occasions, awe-inspiring victory.

Perhaps the greatest of all was Offaly's All-Ireland hurling victory of 1994. It was a day when, from a Limerick point of view, the gods were in a wicked mood.

With 5 minutes to go, Limerick were leading, by 2:13 to 1:11, having played their best hurling since their first-round victory over Cork. On the other hand, Offaly were having their poorest game of the season and Limerick seemed likely to capture their eighth All-Ireland crown. Having regained the lead in the fifth minute of the game, Limerick never allowed Offaly to forge ahead and, as the game moved towards the closing five minutes, they held a 5-point lead.

At that point the Offaly trainer Eamonn Cregan, himself a former Limerick hurler, dismayed at his team's hitherto dismal display had, in his own mind, conceded defeat. Yet he still urged on his charges as he paced the sideline.

All of a sudden, Limerick were struck with a bolt from the blue in the form of an Offaly scoring spree. A seemingly unnecessary foul on Billy Dooley brought Offaly a 21-yard free to the right of the Limerick goal. Contrary to instructions from the sideline, Billy's brother, Johnny, went for a goal — and got it. Within 55 seconds the sliotar was back again in the Limerick net from the hurley of Pat O'Connor. In the remaining minutes, Offaly added a further five points. Over the seventy minutes of the match the Dooley brothers scored a joint total of 2:11— Johnny 1:4; Joe 1:2; Billy 0:5 — final score: Offaly 3:16; Limerick 2:13.

It was a fairy-tale ending for Offaly - a sort of miracle. In a way it reminded me of what I used see on the cinema screen in my youth, when Joe Palooka, in the boxing ring, would absorb a fierce pounding and battering up to the final round. Then he would cut loose and produce a devastating grandstand finish and a knockout victory.

In defeat, a stunned Limerick had a nightmare from which to recover. In victory, Offaly, as always, were dignified and didn't hide their sense of sympathy for the vanquished Limerick men.

The following are some samples of what the sportswriters had to say the following day:

Sometimes victory is as bewildering as defeat. When with a wave of an ash wand a five-point deficit turns into a six-point winning margin you need to rub your eyes a little and look out for the sleight of hand that has deceived the brain. Offaly trooped in off the Croke Park turf yesterday holding the silverware but grasping very little else. Winners have seldom seemed so subdued. The thrill of larceny differs from the thrill of the struggle.

Tom Humphries, *The Irish Times.*

In all of my years reporting hurling for this newspaper, or before it, I've never seen such a dramatic finish to an All-Ireland final. Limerick looked winners almost all the way at Croke Park yesterday and then, hey presto, they were defeated. Gone — relegated to second best in a splendid game. It was as if a fairy godmother, or some magician, waved a magic wand for Offaly and then they were winners — winners of the county's third All-Ireland title in 13 years.

Everyone in an attendance of 56,458 was stunned by the sudden upheaval of the game in the last five minutes ... like many more neutral observers of a great final I almost wept when Limerick lost.

They were so much superior for so long that it seemed impossible that they could lose. And then, as if a switch were turned off, the lights went out and they were gone. Dead.... But no matter how well Limerick played, Offaly won. So, it must be conceded that, for whatever reason on the day, Offaly were the better team. They certainly didn't look it for a long time. But they must get full marks for sticking in there when all seemed lost and then, when the chance came, taking it with open arms.

Paddy Downey, The Irish Times

The victory, Offaly's third senior hurling success, was the result of a miracle of such proportions that it defies Biblical analogy. Damn it, it almost defies description.... If Limerick had been more economical with their use of the enormous amount of possession they enjoyed, they would have been out of reach at half-time. The tricky breeze can only be partly to blame for the 12 wides they struck in that first half, six of those coming in the opening twelve minutes.

Donal Keenan, Irish Independent.

Limerick had unravelled so savagely on the edge of victory, their pain was frightening. Not the customary, long-faced regret of a beaten All-Ireland team. This was harsher, somehow more daunting.

Goalkeeper, Joe Quaid, remembered asking an umpire how much time remained just before Johnny Dooley ignited the uprising. Six minutes, he was told.

'Ah, six minutes,' thought Joe. 'that'll go quick enough.'

Damn sure it would.

Vincent Hogan, Irish Independent

Unbelievable, mind-boggling, sensational, incredible, unforgettable. Trot out all the descriptive tags that might spring to mind and they still wouldn't do justice to one of the most amazing All-Ireland hurling finals ever witnessed at Croke Park.

The heroes were Offaly and their luckless victims Limerick, who must still be wondering how they allowed a match, which they dominated and controlled for virtually 65 minutes, to slip from their grasp in an unforgettable closing five-minute spell....

Not for many, many years, has one team dominated an All-Ireland occasion to the extent that Limerick did and still walk away empty-handed.... There was no denying that Limerick looked a team of all the talents from an early stage and while they were not allowed to perform to the heights achieved against Antrim they appeared to be in command in most sectors.... The rest will go down in hurling history as a gallant Offaly side committed grand larceny in defying all the odds to bring off the greatest recovery operation ever witnessed on a hurling field.

Seán Ó Ceallacháin, *Evening Press*

Quite frankly, I find it impossible to rationalise just how they let this All-Ireland title slip from a seemingly impregnable position with just five minutes remaining.

Offaly deserve enormous credit for coming back from the precipice, but surely the story of this extraordinary game just has to be Limerick's amazing collapse ... men like Ciaran Carey, Ger Hegarty and Mike Houlihan are entitled to ask what more they could have done in trying to earn the county their first All-Ireland title since '73. All three were nothing short of majestic.

Nicky English, *Irish Independent*

The green-and-white army shuffled up to the Canal Bridge in almost total silence.

They were goal-shocked and point-shocked and heartbroken and mind broken — this was sport at its most cruel.

On the way down to the City centre I met some Offaly folk — they too were almost silent.

For once I fully appreciated what it is to be dumbfounded....

Johnny (Dooley) cast logic to the wind and drove the ball low into the net.

Suddenly Limerick's lead of five points was down to two — the rope had become alarmingly thin.

A minute later that rope was in shreds. Limerick fought back bravely — but for them Offaly were The Fateful County.

And you couldn't help feeling that it had all been scripted by those pranksome gods who sometimes seem to preside over sport. Those late five points seemed the stuff of dreams; for Offaly they were like manna — for Limerick they were like arrows piercing the soul.

And followers of the green-and-white will — when they recover their minds — argue that Offaly's three goals were tinged with good fortune.

And perhaps they were — many goals in hurling are.

The first came in the 4th minute, Joe Quaid parried Johnny Dooley's penalty; Joe Dooley pounced like a hawk on a chicken too far from her mother.

The 21 yards free that brought goal number two was not a rocket in the style of Nicky Rackard — it stole in between two camáns.

The third goal came after a long ball that bounced twice before Pat O'Connor cut it to the net from 12 yards....

And then Johnny Dooley's moment of inspiration made Offaly's desert flower — soon it became The Promised Land.

When Limerick's tragedy is coolly analysed, two factors will stand out. They perpetrated 18 wides, many from very good positions. And they overdid the passing; sometimes they passed when a shot would have made more sense.

Con Houlihan, *Evening Press*

As we enter the hurling world of the new millennium, it would seem inappropriate, in a chapter on Offaly, not to devote a piece to Brian Whelehan. Brian is an extremely talented and gifted hurler who has acquired legendary status during his playing career. He was recently selected at right half-back on the Hurling Team of the Millennium and is the only present-day player to have been be given this honour.

I remember standing on the embankment at Nowlan Park, Kilkenny, watching the All-Ireland under-21 final between Offaly and Waterford, in 1992. Early in the first half my wife, Mary, turned to me and said: 'There's the best man on the field', pointing to Brian Whelehan in the Offaly half-back line. She was new to hurling games but having played hockey at school, she never had difficulty in identifying a quality player.

Brian was born in 1971. His greatest hurling displays have been given in defence but he showed that he could do great and inspirational things at full forward too, at Croke Park on All-Ireland final day in 1998. With a personal tally of 1:6 to his credit, he was honoured with the Man-of-the-Match accolade on that occasion.

He won All-Ireland minor titles in 1987 and 1989 and made his senior début when he came on as a substitute against Antrim in the All-Ireland semi-final of 1989.

All of the major hurling honours have come his way; a Railway Cup and National League title; All-Star Awards in 1992, 1995 and 1998; All-Ireland titles in 1994 and 1998; All-Ireland club titles with Birr in 1995 and 1998; Texaco Hurler of the Year in 1994 and 1998, thus following in the footsteps of fellow countymen Pat Delaney and Eugene Coughlan who were Texaco Hurlers of the Year in 1981 and 1985 respectively. Brian became the first hurler since the inception of that award, in 1958, to be honoured with it twice.

Brian Whelehan is an immensely talented hurler with a particular flair for the big occasion. A ball player, and a true sportsman, he is a master of the basics and is magnificent at sweeping and covering in defence.

His family is steeped in hurling. His brothers, Simon and Barry, are county senior colleagues. His father, Pa Joe, gave great service to Offaly but had departed the scene by the time that success came Offaly's way at the beginning of the 1980s.

Writing in *The Irish Times*, on the day after the 1998 hurling final, Tom Humphries in an article on Brian had this to say:

> *They should kit Brian Whelehan out properly for once and for all. Superheroes shouldn't wear the same drab garb as the rest of us. Give him some rubber gear and a cloak and make him the Caped Crusader, damn it. He shouldn't just be number five.*
>
> *He was named Man-of-the-Match yesterday but after twenty minutes it was looking like a cliff-hanger from the old matinee days. Whelehan tied to the tracks with the steam engine bearing down on him. Toot! Toot!*
>
> *The bench switched Whelehan to attack and he scored the goal that broke Kilkenny's spirit having earlier made the block which kept his team alive.*
>
> *It should be noted of course that he started the game with a dose of influenza which would have killed a horse and finished the game with a torn hamstring.*

Brian Whelehan

The move to the forwards worked like a tonic. It was the second time in this antic Summer that he has made that novel journey. On each occasion his fortunes and those of his team have been reversed.

His presence lubricated the machinery of the Offaly forward line.

For twenty minutes they had clanked and clunked and they tried to manufacture scores. Whelehan put himself at the centre of the process, first as an adventurous wing forward, then as a full forward.... On his greatest day he insists on pushing the laurels elsewhere. Superhero stuff.

LIMERICK'S FAMOUS FIVE-IN-A-ROW

As the 1930s dawned, the sun was setting on a great era of Cork hurling. At that time, Kilkenny were the emerging team and were to go on to greatness in that decade. However, by 1933, a new hurling power had appeared on the horizon. It was Limerick.

Limerick dominated the 1930s by the sheer strength and magnetism of their hurling play and hurling men. They played a delightful brand of hurling — classical stuff of fire, verve and élan that captured the public imagination and brought the crowds flocking to see Limerick play. Little wonder then that the team was in such demand, particularly for church-building tournaments. Jackie Power used say to Mick Mackey, 'There must be a place in heaven for us Mick — we have helped build so many churches'.

The Limerick team of that era had a glamour that enthralled the crowd. Above all, they had a flair for the big occasion. They had epic encounters with all the leading hurling counties. The players' names spelt hurling magic and when Limerick faced Kilkenny, in the All-Ireland final of 1936, the attendance of 51,235 spectators was a record for a hurling final. It was also the first time, in the history of the GAA, that attendance at the hurling final exceeded that at the football final.

In 1933, a great All-Ireland campaign, which ended in a Titanic struggle with Kilkenny (Kilkenny 1:7; Limerick 0:6), blooded Limerick for the glory days that lay around the corner. That was the final that was remembered for Johnny Dunne's famous goal. It was also this final that prompted Jack Rochford, a Kilkenny great of earlier years, to express the view that the Limerick side of 1933 was the best team he had ever seen come out of Munster — and he wondered how they had lost to Kilkenny on this occasion.

In the period from 15 October 1933 to 24 April 1938, Limerick played sixty-five games — in Ireland, England and America. They won fifty-eight of them, drew four and lost only three. It was a performance in consistency that had greatness written all over it.

It was the Mackey era, and Mick, the darling of the crowd, stamped his personality and hurling brilliance indelibly on it.

Limerick won four Munster titles in a row: 1933–1936, inclusive. In those years, they contested all four All-Ireland finals and won two of them. In 1933, Limerick lost to Kilkenny; in 1935 another clash of the Titans was lost, by one point, to a great Kilkenny team which was led by Lory Meagher.

Lory's counsel to his men as they faced the favourites, Limerick, on a day of atrocious weather conditions was: 'Keep it on the ground, pull first time, keep it moving'.

In the years 1934-1938, inclusive, four of the five Railway Cup competitions were won by Munster teams that were dominated by Limerick men. In the 1936 competition, with Mick Mackey as captain, eleven Limerick men wore the Munster jersey.

Now to the famous five! I refer of course to Limerick's National League victories — five in a row in the competitions during the years 1933–38. This achievement established a record that, up to the time of writing, has never since been equalled.

The following is a brief overview of the five campaigns:

Victories over Tipperary, Offaly and Clare saw Limerick qualify for the final of the 1933–34 National League, against Dublin, who were a formidable force throughout much of the 1930s. The game was played at the Gaelic Grounds before an attendance of 10,000 people. Limerick, who were captained by Mick Kennedy (a Tipperary man who hailed from The Rag, near Thurles town), won a great contest by 3:6 to 3:3. The star of the thirty players was John Mackey, at wing forward — the greatest of his era in that position. Without his contribution and brilliance, Limerick might well have lost.

The following year, Limerick faced Kilkenny in the final at Nowlan Park. Limerick had qualified with a clean sheet — a draw with Cork, in Croom, and victory in all of their other games. The final of the 1934–35 League turned out to be one of the classics of hurling — plenty of crisp ground-striking and close, manly tackling. It was thrill-a-minute stuff with Limerick grimly holding on to a two-point lead to win by 1:6 to 1:4. That League campaign saw two future greats emerge into the limelight: Jackie Power and Paddy McMahon.

Limerick faced Dublin at Croke Park for the 1935–36 decider. Their route to the final that season was taken via victories over Laois, Clare, Waterford, Tipperary, Galway, Kilkenny and Cork. Captained by midfielder, Timmy Ryan, they won a hard-fought contest by 7:2 to 4:4. This now made Limerick's total three in a row. Even better days were still to come.

In the 1936–37 League competition, Limerick suffered their only defeat in five years of league matches. Playing without Mick Ryan, John Mackey and Mick Mackey, they lost to Tipperary, at Thurles, by 4:5 to 2:4. However, they got back on the winning trail again with wins over Laois, Waterford, Galway, Kilkenny and Dublin. Following a draw with Clare they faced Cork in the final, at the Gaelic Grounds. We can only speculate as to what kind of a game it was, for the final score was a most unusual one: Limerick 11:6; Cork 5:1.

Hard-earned victories over Waterford, Cork, Clare and Kilkenny saw Limerick qualify for the National League final of 1937–38, against their old rivals Tipperary, at Thurles, before a record crowd of over 15,000 spectators.

Limerick had a score to settle, for Tipperary had beaten them in a superb Munster final in 1937; and settle the score they did with a convincing 5:2 to 1:1 win. Peter Cregan, an outstanding minor centre back of 1935 and 1936, established himself on the senior team during this League championship and went on to prove himself as one of the great hurling defenders of the following ten years.

Limerick finished the 1930s with a smashing victory over All-Ireland champions, Kilkenny, in the first Oireachtas Tournament. This was played at Croke Park, in the late Autumn, and the final score read: Limerick 4:4; Kilkenny 2:5.

Limerick entered the 1940s on a winning note — a Munster title, after a gruelling campaign (an epic draw and replay with Waterford, an epic draw and replay with Cork); an All-Ireland title, after a semi-final win over Galway; and a 3:7 to 1:7 victory over their arch-rivals, Kilkenny, in the final. It was a year that marked the début of Dick Stokes, a highly talented and brilliant exponent of the hurling craft. Dick had shown his class in the Munster Colleges victory, over Leinster Colleges, in the All-Ireland final of 1939. He would continue to do so in the green jersey of Limerick and the blue jersey of Munster.

A Limerick selection from this era reads like an all-time great line-out:

Paddy Scanlon

Peter Cregan, Tom McCarthy, Mick Kennedy

Mickey Cross, Paddy Clohessy, Garret Howard

Timmy Ryan, Mick Ryan

John Mackey, Mick Mackey, Dick Stokes

Dave Clohessy, Paddy McMahon, Jackie Power

Remainder of panel: Mick Hickey, Jim Roche, Paddy Carroll, Bob McConkey, Ned Cregan.

The Limerick Team of 1935–36

Unique Senior Doubles

Up to the time of writing this book, only two counties have achieved the rare distinction of winning the All-Ireland senior hurling and the All-Ireland senior football titles in the same year. These counties are Tipperary and Cork, both of which had the great honour of achieving 'the double' on two occasions.

Tipperary 1895 — Football

Of the nineteen counties that were affiliated to the GAA in 1895, only ten competed in the championships of that year — one in Ulster, four in Munster and five in Leinster.

In the Munster Championship, Clare gave Waterford a walk-over. Limerick beat Kerry. Tipperary and Limerick then contested the Munster football final. The game was played in Kilmallock, in February 1896, and was preceded by the hurling final. Special trains ferried supporters to the occasion where admission was 3d (old pence).

Limerick (Commercials) were the fancied side. They were still a mighty force and a leading power in Limerick football. They had won the All-Ireland title in the first year of the championships — 1887 — and were destined to win it again in 1896.

In a thrilling game which held the crowd in suspense from start to finish, the issue was in doubt right up to the final whistle. It ended with Tipperary taking their third provincial title on the score of 0:5 to 0:2. It was a proud moment for Tipperary as it was the first occasion since 1887 that they had taken victory over the great Limerick side.

The All-Ireland final of that year was played at Jones's Road, on 15 March 1896. Tipperary, sporting all white, were represented by Arravale Rovers.

Their opponents, Meath, were represented by Pierce O'Mahony's and were clad in crimson and green. On their way to the final, Meath had firstly defeated Cavan, who played in the Leinster championship in 1895 (there was no Ulster championship that year). They then beat Kilkenny, and followed that with a 0:6-to-0:2 victory over Dublin (a game in which it is believed coloured flags were used for the first time by umpires when signalling scores).

A capacity crowd packed the Jones's Road ground on All-Ireland final day 1895. Supporters of both teams were treated to a most sporting display of fast, clean, scientific football, after which Tipperary emerged victorious with a score of 0:4 to 0:3. Man-of-the-Match was Tipperary's Willie Ryan who roamed the pitch and turned in a powerful performance — with Tipperary facing defeat, he followed up a punt ahead, gathered, and scored the equalising point. In the dying moments he scored the winning point also, from a free. It was Tipperary's second All-Ireland football title and on this occasion they were captained by Paddy Finn.

T.F. O'Sullivan recorded the following

'How did Tipperary beat Navan?' Mr P.P. Sutton asked in Sport. *He answered the question himself — first, and overall, there is only one Willie Ryan in Ireland; second, by the length of their kicks; and last, but not least, they were in luck.*

T.F. O.Sullivan continued:

There was an extraordinary sequel to the contest. The referee wrote in the following day's papers stating that the Arravale Rovers secured one of their scores unfairly, and that the match should be played over again. The Central Council, however, upheld the decision given by the referee on the field, awarding the match to Tipperary, but decided to give a set of silver medals to the Navan team as winners of the Leinster championship. Navan, in a most sportsmanlike spirit, through their President (Mr J.P. Timmons) also refused to take advantage of the mistake alleged to have been made by the referee in awarding the match to their opponents. The two teams subsequently met on three occasions to test the question of superiority. Two of the matches resulted in draws, but Tipperary won well on the third meeting.

The members of the victorious Tipperary team were as follows:

*Paddy Finn (Captain), Willie Ryan, Bob Quane, Jim Riordan,
Mick Finn, 'Terry' McInerney, Paddy Glasheen, Jack Carey,
Mick Conroy, Dick Butler, Willie Ryan, Jack Heffernan,
Gerry O'Brien, Paddy Daly, Batt Finn, Phil Dwyer and John Carew.*

Tipperary 1895 — Hurling

In the early stages of the Munster championship of 1895, Waterford got a walk-over from Clare and Limerick defeated Kerry. Cork didn't appear in the Championship, and Waterford appear to have dropped out.

The final was contested by Limerick and Tipperary at Kilmallock, in February 1896. The match was played before the football final which was also contested by the same counties.

Tipperary had an easy win and the final result was: Tipperary (Tubberadora) 7:8; Limerick (St Michael's) 0:2.

A press report on the hurling final read as follows:

Ably led by the strong and fearless Mikey Maher, the style of the Tipperary hurlers was fast, free and open, and their positional work perfect. In every unit there was sting and dash; in every line there was ability and method. With such a gallant combination, it looks as if Tipperary is going to make some history in the ancient pastime.

The All-Ireland final of 1895 was also played on the same day, and at the same venue, as the football final — 15 March 1896, at Jones's Road. Represented by a famed Tubberadora selection Tipperary were captained by Mikey Maher — affectionately called 'Big Mikey' and known, honoured and revered throughout the hurling world. They had a runaway victory over Tullaroan from Kilkenny who, before the game, wouldn't hear of defeat. The final score was Tipperary: 6:8; Kilkenny: 1:0. It is said that P.J. Riordan of Drumbane got all of the Tipperary scores.

Mikey Maher was the first man to lead a hurling team to three All-Ireland successes when he captained Tipperary again in 1896 and 1898.

The Tubberadora team that represented Tipperary in 1895

There was also another famous hurler on the victorious 1895 team —
Denis Walsh. He won his first All-Ireland medal that year and 21 years
later, in 1916, he won his fifth when Tipperary beat Kilkenny. In the
intervening years he won the other three medals in 1896, 1898 and 1899.

The press report quoted above was indeed prophetic. Having won
the All-Ireland hurling title in 1895, Tipperary repeated the success in
1896, and then went on to take further victories — three in a row — in
1898, 1899 and 1900.

The victorious Tipperary hurling team of 1895 were as follows:

Mikey Maher (Captain), Denis Walsh, Johnny Walsh, Ned Maher,
Jim Flanagan, Tim Flanagan, Jack Connolly, Jack Maher,
Ned Brennan, John Maher, Bill Devane, Phil Byrne, Peter Maher,
Will Kerwick, Paddy Riordan, Jim Gleeson, Fergus Moriarty.

Tipperary 1900 — Football

In 1900, Tipperary made a good start to the century by repeating
double' for the second time.

That year, the draws in the Munster championships, for both codes,
were as follows:

Tipperary v Cork

Limerick v Clare

Kerry were awarded a bye into both finals.

Tipperary's (Clonmel Shamrocks) first-round game against Cork (Fermoy) was a close affair. Cork led at half-time by 1 point — the only score of the first half. Tipperary displayed more attacking ideas in the second half and, with their defence holding firm, they won by 0:3 points to 0:1.

They then faced Limerick (Commercials) in the semi-final. This was going to be a key test of their worth and ability. They held the Limerick champions in the highest regard but, undaunted, they rose to the occasion in splendid fashion. Spurred on by a super display by Bob Quane, who was a member of the 1895 All-Ireland winning team, they emerged the winners of a game that had been packed with thrills and heroics. The final score was Tipperary 2:4; Limerick 2:1.

The road was now clear for a first-ever Munster final meeting between the premier county and the men from the Kingdom, who incidentally had at this time yet to win an All-Ireland football crown. Kerry, represented by the famed Laune Rangers, were perceived as slight favourites in some quarters. They opened in devastating form and quickly ran up an early lead. But Tipperary settled, tightened their defence, took a grip on the game and finished with a convincing 1:14-to-1:4 victory.

In the All-Ireland semi-final, Tipperary came face to face with their Leinster neighbours Kilkenny (Slatequarry Miners), at Carrick-on-Suir. On this occasion, Tipperary lost the contest by 2 points: 1:6 to 0:7. They then lodged an objection on the grounds that Kilkenny had had the assistance of men who were from Tipperary. Central Council upheld the objection; Tipperary, however, offered to replay the match but Kilkenny refused to take part and so Tipperary were awarded a walk-over.

The All-Ireland home final of 1900 wasn't played until 21 September 1902 when Tipperary met Galway (Tuam), at Terenure. Galway had received a walk-over from the Ulster champions, Antrim, in the semi-final.

The full-time score of 2:17 to 0:1, in the All-Ireland home final, speaks for the Munster team's superiority over a Tuam team that decided to go it alone rather than pick a team representative of the entire county. Such an option had become available to all county championship winners following a rule change at the 1891 annual convention, held on 13 January 1892.

The victory against Galway paved the way to the 1900 All-Ireland final at Jones's Road, on 26 October 1902. Tipperary, led by their captain, John Tobin of Clonmel Shamrocks, beat the London side (Hibernians), by 3:7 to 0:2, in a game that preceded the hurling final of that year.

The victorious Tipperary football team were:

Jack Tobin, Bill McRell, Pat Maloney, Jack Dwan, Davy Myers, Mick Walsh, Jack O'Brien, Davy Smyth, Paul Cox, Jim Cooney, Pat Wall, Dan Harney, Bill O'Toole, Jack Shea, Bob Quane, Dick Hourigan, and Jack Hayes.

Tipperary 1900 — Hurling

Tipperary's (Two Mile Borris) first-round game against Cork (Redmonds) at Dungarvan was a rip-roaring affair. There was some great hurling and many brilliant passages of play. The score was level on five occasions. Behind at half time by 0:7 to 0:5, Tipperary finished the stronger of the two teams and won by 0:12 points to 0:9.

Tipperary then went on to meet Clare (Tulla) in the Munster semi-final, which was played in Limerick. The first quarter of the match was close and exciting, but when Tipperary moved into overdrive it all became one-way traffic. They scored at will and the final score tells its own story: Tipperary (Two Mile Borris) 6:11; Clare (Tulla) 1:6.

The Munster final against Kerry (Kilmoyley) was almost a replica of the Clare game. Down only 5 points at half-time, Kerry collapsed before the sheer power and class of Tipperary in the second half. They were, no doubt, glad to hear the final whistle. The final result was, Tipperary 6:11; Kerry 2:1 (although some records show the Kerry score as 1:9).

Tipperary's next outing was the All-Ireland semi-final against Kilkenny (Mooncoin). This match has since been described as a

Homeric struggle, and it is comparable to Tipperary's first-round contest with Cork in the Munster championship. Mooncoin, with a selection that included Tullaroan and Threecastles men, were leading at the interval by 1:6 to 0:4. However, Tipperary had by far the better of the second half, outscoring their opponents by 10 points to 2. They finished with a narrow, but merited, win on the score of 1:11 to 1:8.

The home final, which was played in Terenure on 21 September 1902, was a tame enough affair. Galway (Ardrahan) couldn't match the experience and overall superiority of the Tipperary men who emerged victorious on the final score of 6:13 to 1:5.

Then came the All-Ireland final, on 26 October 1902, against London (Redmonds) — a powerful band of Irish emigrants who worked in London. With Ned Hayes leading great names such as Mikey Maher, Tom Semple and Jack Gleeson, Tipperary, perceived in many quarters to be well-nigh invincible, almost met their Waterloo. Entering the last five minutes of the match they trailed by 6 points to 5 and their reign as champions appeared to be over. Then disaster struck for London. Their captain, Dan Horgan, moved to clear a loose ball and, expecting it to hop, he put his hand to the ground only to find it had stuck in a rut where he accidentally touched it.

From the resultant free taken by captain Ned Hayes, the Tipperary forwards rushed in to bundle the London defenders — ball and all — over the goal-line. They took further advantage from a weak puck-out and scored again. Then it was all over — final score: Tipperary 2:5; London 0:6. It was Tipperary's sixth title and the victory gave them a three-in-a-row All-Ireland success, a triumph which Cork had first achieved in the years 1892, 1893 and 1894.

Thus did Tipperary establish a record that no other county has ever emulated, and with present-day arrangements, one can never see their record being equalled. On each occasion in 1895 and 1900 they won the double on the same day and at the same venue — the dates, 15 March 1896 and 26 October 1902; the venue, Jones's Road. The celebrations must have been very special indeed.

After the two finals of 26 October 1902, the hurling and football teams of Tipperary and London were entertained to dinner by the Lord Mayor at the Mansion House. Also present were Alderman Jim

Nowlan, President of the GAA, and Luke O'Toole, the Association's Secretary.

The victorious hurling team were:

Ned Hayes (Captain), Mattie Ryan, Billy Maher, Tom Allen, Matt Purcell, Paddy 'Best' Maher, Paddy Hayes, Mike Wall, Bill Gleeson, Jack Gleeson, Billy Gleeson, Jim Keeffe, Mikey Maher, Ned Maher, Johnny Walsh, Tommy Ryan and Tom Semple.

Cork 1890 — Football

The year of 1890 is memorable as being the year that the GAA Central Council strongly approved an appeal to its members, by their patron Archbishop Croke, to join the Temperance Movement, as the Centenary of Fr Matthew approached. It was also the year that Cork (Midleton) led the way in the field of 'the double'.

On 19 October 1890, in a replay of the Munster football final, in Banteer, they beat Kerry (Laune Rangers) by 1:4 to 0:1. (They had already beaten Waterford by 0:6 to 0:0.) The first game against Kerry, played in Limerick on 28 September, was abandoned with less than five minutes of the match remaining. Neither of the teams had scored at that stage and we are told that the football then burst and could not be replaced.

At the All-Ireland semi-finals that year, Cork had defeated the Ulster champions, Armagh (Armagh Harps), by 1:15 to nil, in Clonturk on 12 June 1892. In the meantime, Wexford (Blues and Whites) had taken a walk-over from Galway (Caherlistrane), the Connaught champions of that year.

The All-Ireland final of 1890 wasn't played until 26 June 1892. On this occasion, Cork (Midleton) beat Wexford (Blue and Whites) by 2:4 to 0:1. Cork were captained by Jim Power, their goalkeeper and the game was refereed by J.J. Kenny from Dublin.

The delay in playing the final was due in the main to the failure of the teams to meet on the dates fixed by the Central Council. Wexford's rather poor performance centred around the fact that, ' ... the team had been practically dissolved for 18 months, and had only a fortnight's training for the final.'

Cork 1890 — Hurling

The Cork hurlers had already won the All-Ireland hurling crown by the time the football final of 1890 was played. Prior to that, they had beaten Kerry (Kilmoyley) in the Munster final, in Limerick on 28 September, by 2:0 to 0:1. The 1890 All-Ireland final took place in Clonturk on 16 November. Aughabullogue represented Cork; they played barefooted, and were dressed in white jerseys and breeches and green caps. They were a team of speed merchants. Their opponents were Wexford, represented by Castlebridge, who had come through a Leinster campaign with wins over Kilkenny, Dublin and Laois without conceding a goal.

T.F. O'Sullivan, writing on the final, gives us an insight into what kind of game it was: 'The hurling contest was very rough. The Castlebridge men played a reckless game.'

The match was unfinished. At half-time, Cork led by 1:3 to 1 point but an early second-half rally saw Wexford score 2 goals and 1 point after which Cork added 3 more points. The score then stood at Wexford 2:2; Cork 1:6. Under the rules of the game at that time, Wexford were ahead because no number of points equalled a goal. With 10 minutes remaining, the trouble came to a head and Cork, alleging rough play by their opponents, left the field. Following the report of referee John Sheehy, of Limerick, the match was awarded to Cork, on a 3-to-2 vote, at a meeting of the Central Council.

Cork 1990 — Football

All the foregoing achievements have long passed from living memory. Only the 'béaloideas' lives on. On the other hand, however, Cork's second All-Ireland senior double is well remembered. It happened in 1990, exactly one hundred years after the first Cork All-Ireland double. It was a very special year for Teddy McCarthy who wrote himself into GAA folklore by becoming the only player to accomplish the senior double in the same year. He played at centrefield on the hurling team, and at left half-forward with the footballers.

Teddy, a great dual player, was born in July 1965 and had had a very impressive record at underage level before he entered the senior ranks.

The victory of 1990 was also the first time that Cork won two All-Ireland football titles in a row; and on each occasion they did it without scoring a goal in the final. The results were:

1989 — Cork 0:17; Mayo 1:11

1990 — Cork 0:11; Meath 0:9.

Indeed, Cork might well have won three in a row for they had only missed a victory by one point, against Meath, in a replay of the 1988 All-Ireland football final.

From 1987 onwards, Cork had a very talented panel of players. For four consecutive years they had beaten Kerry in the Munster final and really showed their class and superiority in 1990 with a 2:23-to-1:11 victory over the men from the Kingdom.

Roscommon fell to Cork in the All-Ireland semi-final of 1990 on the score of 0:17 to 0:10. Meath's victory over Donegal, in the second semi-final, a week later, brought yet another All-Ireland confrontation between these counties.

Cork were all too conscious of their 1987 and 1988 All-Ireland defeats at the hands of Meath. In addition, they were acutely aware of Meath's victory over them in the 1990 League semi-final played the previous April. That match had finished with a score of Meath 0:14; Cork 0:10. Meath had then gone on to take the League title with a 2-point win over Down. These factors gave Meath an added incentive to complete the double — the All-Ireland and National League titles — as they had done in 1988.

The question was, could Cork find the scoring power to overcome the granite-like grit of their arch rivals, Meath? The final wasn't a game for the purists. There was very little free-flowing football. Close physical contact led to a degree of friction among the players and just before half-time, Cork lost their full forward, Colm O'Neill, when he was sidelined.

On this occasion, however, it was Cork who dug deepest and took the title. Kildare-born and former Kildare player, Larry Tompkins, captained Cork to the All-Ireland victory and took the Sam Maguire Cup back to Cork and his club, Castlehaven.

It was Cork's sixth title — an overdue, well-fashioned and well-deserved victory. The winning team in the final lined out as follows:

John Kerins

Tony Nation, Stephen O'Brien, Niall Cahalane

Michael Slocum, Conor Counihan, Barry Coffey

Shay Fahy, Danny Culloty

Dave Barry, Larry Tompkins, Teddy McCarthy

Paul McGrath, Colm O'Neill, Mick McCarthy.

Playing substitutes: John O'Driscoll, Paddy Hayes and John Cleary replaced Mick McCarthy, Dave Barry and Paul McGrath respectively.

Cork 1990 — Hurling

In 1990, the path to glory for Cork hurlers read as follows:

Cork 3:16; Kerry 3:7 — 25 May, in Tralee

Cork 4:15; Waterford 1:8 —3 June, in Thurles

Cork 4:16; Tipperary 2:14 — 15 July, in Thurles

Cork 2:20; Antrim 1:13 — 5th August, in Croke Park

Cork 5:15 Galway 2:21 — 2 September, in Croke Park.

In Cork's Munster final win over Tipperary, two performances stood out from a fine overall team effort. The first came from six-foot-plus centre forward Mark Foley, from Timoleague. Mark found the net when he doubled on a sideline cut-in just on the stroke of half-time and Cork adjourned for the break only 2 points in arrears. Mark finished the game with a personal tally of 2:7.

The second display of outstanding skill came in the second half of the match. Jim Cashman, at centre half-back, was majestic in blotting out the potential threat posed by Tipperary centre forward, Declan Ryan.

Thomas Mulcahy

Teddy McCarthy

Larry Tompkins

A good team, with the centre half-back and centre forward producing top class performances is always likely to come out on top — and so it was with Cork in that Munster final.

The 1990 All-Ireland hurling final was not the same kind of game as the provincial final had been — equally brilliant and exciting — but still very different. Galway folk will still analyse the final of 1990 and wonder how their team lost it. Although they conceded a 'soft' goal very early on, they were the dominant force for much of the game. However, the Fates were against them that day. This was confirmed when a great save by Ger Cunningham was deflected over the end line and was then signalled by the umpire as a wide instead of a 'seventy'.

Cork's concentration on doing the basics well, won the day. Vital goals came from their solid ground hurling which proved very decisive at key stages in the match.

In a superb final Cork had twenty scores and Galway twenty-three; but when converted to points, the final tally read 30 points to 27, in Cork's favour.

In the 1990 All-Ireland hurling final there were forty-three scores in all as compared to 100 years earlier, when the 1890 final produced just eleven, despite the fact that the scoring areas was significantly larger at that time.

The winning Cork team in the 1990 final, captained by Thomas Mulcahy, a most accomplished forward, lined out as follows:

Ger Cunningham

John Considine, Denis Walsh, Seanie O'Gorman

Sean McCarthy, Jim Cashman, Kieran McGuckian

Brendan O'Sullivan, Teddy McCarthy

Ger Fitzgerald, Mark Foley, Tony O'Sullivan

Thomas Mulcahy, Kevin Hennessy, John Fitzgibbon.

To complete the senior double in a given year is a wonderful achievement. Very few countries have the capacity or the potential even to contemplate it.

We have seen that since the start of the Championships, in 1887, up to the present day, the double has been won on only four occasions and by only two counties.

Based on present-day form, I would rate the following counties — and in the order listed — as being the most likely to achieve the double: Cork, Galway, Offaly.

However, they would need a fair share of luck along the way in order to do so.

CAMOGIE

Camogie derives its name from the Irish word camóg which means a stick with a crook at the end of it.

The origins of the game go back to 1903. Camogie was developed by lady members of the Dublin Keatings branch of the Gaelic League who set about providing some suitable form of outdoor exercise for Irish girls. The driving force behind the establishment of this new movement was Máire Ní Chinnéide BA

The rules of the game were drawn up by the committee of the Keating Camóguidheacht Club with the assistance of some members of the Keating Hurling Club. The size of the playing pitch was set at minimum 45x60 yards, and maximum 60x100 yards. One interesting rule was that intentionally stopping the ball with the skirt was a foul. Teams lined out 12 a side and, unlike hurling, camogie was a strictly non-physical-contact sport.

The first inter-club camóguidheacht match was played in the County Meath Agricultural Gardens at Navan, on Sunday, 17 July 1904, between the Keatings and the Cúchullains clubs (Cúchullains were the second club to be formed in Dublin). The game was run in connection with An Aeridheacht ('An Entertainment in the open').

The Freeman's Journal carried the following report of the match:

Both teams were attired in graceful costumes. The Cúchullains wore light blue blouses with red sashes and the Keatings also wore light blue, with yellow ties, the colours of the branch. At the opening of the game all the players occupied their allotted places in the field, and the ball was thrown in by the referee, Mr Bradley, between the centres, thus ensuring good open play from the start. The game was fast throughout and it was within five minutes of the call of time before the first score was recorded — a goal by the Keating club. For several minutes before the score was made, the Keatings were playing up to the Cúchullains goal, and a feature of the game was the splendid defence of Miss Lombard, the Cúchullain full back.

The spread of the game was slow but steady. In 1912, Sliabh Ruadh reported as follows:

> *The camogie association has been making steady progress for some years past and the following is a list of the affiliated clubs: Dublin 11, London 2, Wexford 5, Meath 2. Louth 2. Other counties are reported to be coming in as well.*
>
> *The following are the officers for the year 1912: President, The Countess of Fingal, Vice-Presidents, Mrs Hamilton and Mrs O'Nolan. (Máire de Bhuitléir) Organiser, Cáit Ní Dhonncadha.'*

The Dominican Convent, Muckross Park, Donnybrook, Dublin, was the first educational establishment to take up camogie.

The foregoing outlines the tiny acorn from which the camogie organisation sprouted.

By 1932 sufficient progress had been made to enable an All-Ireland senior camogie championship get under way. In the final of that year, Dublin defeated Galway by 3:2 to 0:2 and became the first holders of the O'Duffy Cup. At that time a game of camogie lasted for 40 minutes. In 1934 the playing period was extended to 50 minutes and remained thus until 1988 when inter-county matches were further extended to 60 minutes. For four decades Dublin were a major power and by 1966 had captured twenty-five All-Ireland titles. They won their last title in 1984 and at the time of writing Dublin lead the field with a total of twenty-six All-Ireland victories.

Cork were prominent until the early 1940s and only came to the forefront again in the 1970s. They rank second in the honours list with a tally of nineteen All-Ireland titles.

Great work has been done in County Antrim. The ladies from the Glens have contested sixteen All-Ireland finals — winning six in all.

Kilkenny began hitting the limelight in the 1970s and between 1974 and 1994 produced outstanding players and brilliant teams that brought a dozen All-Ireland crowns to the Noreside.

In all, seven counties have won All-Ireland titles at senior level: Dublin, Cork, Kilkenny, Antrim, Wexford, Galway and Tipperary. A further six have reached the final — Limerick, Waterford, Down, Derry, Mayo and Louth.

From inception camogie was a game of 12 a-side. However, that all changed with the All-Ireland championship of 1999 when teams lined out 15 a-side just like their hurling counterparts. And what a final it was that year. The contestants were Kilkenny, modern kingpins of the game, and Tipperary, seven times losers since their first final appearance. That was in 1949 and they were still desperately seeking a first All-Ireland crown.

Kilkenny went into the final as firm favourites — and understandably so. In the semi-final a rather fortuitous last-minute goal from a far-out free gave them victory over Cork who had won the last two All-Ireland titles.

On the other hand, Tipperary had taken a terrible trouncing from Cork in the league final — Cork 9:19; Tipperary 2:7. It was a game to be forgotten but it did have a positive side; it bred grim resolve. Tipperary, on All-Ireland final day, were a re-invigorated outfit. From the throw-in, when Dublin referee, Áine Derham got the final underway, they tore into the game with zeal and zest. They played with abandon and élan, spread the ball wide, and ran, and ran, and ran.

Pat Roche, writing in *The Irish Times*, opened his report on the game as follows:

> *A young and eager Tipperary team wrote a defining chapter in the history of the game by winning their first All-Ireland senior title with style and panache before a crowd of 15,084 at Croke Park yesterday. The attendance included President Mary McAleese and the Taoiseach, Bertie Ahern. The last camogie final of the Millennium was marked by a high standard of play, which reflected how well the game has progressed over the years. In an absorbing and often spectacular match, the issue was not finally decided until well into injury time by a pointed free from Tipperary's second-half substitute, Caitriona Hennessy.*

In bringing off this famous victory, all of the Tipperary players emerged as heroines. The half-back line of Meadhbh Stokes, Ciara Gaynor and Sinead Nealon formed the bulwark on which many a

Kilkenny attack floundered. Deirdre Hughes, at full forward, was elusive and brilliant and sent over a series of valuable and spectacular points. She was Sportstar of the week, and her points were described as collector's items. Noelle Kennedy's sharp-shooting brought a total of five points to Tipperary's tally and, when accuracy deserted her, substitute Caitriona Hennessy displayed the coolness of a veteran in scoring 2 points. The second of Catriona's points was the winner and the final score was: Tipperary 0:12; Killkenny 1:8.

The Tipperary Team of 1999

Kilkenny were in the game with a real chance of winning right up to the final whistle. However, victory eluded them despite the sterling efforts of top players such as Sinead Millea, Gillian Dillon and, veteran of 100 battles, Ann Downey, who was sprung from the substitute's bench. All of these players were daughters of famous sons of Kilkenny hurling but, even so, they had to give way to a rampant Tipperary outfit.

The jubilation at the call of time was a delight to behold. The old Irish adage encapsulated it all - 'An rud is annamh is iontach'

Donie Nealon and Len Gaynor, Tipperary hurling stars of yesteryear, would have watched the performance and success of their daughters, Sinead and Ciara, with great pride. At the same time Tipperary stars of more recent days, Michael Cleary and Colm Bonnar, would reflect with deep satisfaction on their contribution to the training and preparation of the team.

It was a great day too for Tipperary's manager, Biddy Phillips, who said: 'It is marvellous for the county, a first senior title, everyone's dream.'

The team returned to the premier county to a rapturous welcome, bearing with them a hat-trick of firsts:

- they won the first 15-a-side final
- they took the O'Duffy Cup to Tipperary for the first time
- they won the first All-Ireland played on a full-length GAA pitch.

The victorious team lined-out as follows:

Jovita Delaney

Siobhan Kelly, Una O'Dwyer, Claire Madden

Meadhbh Stokes, Ciara Gaynor, Sinead Nealon

Emily Hayden, Angela McDermott

Noelle Kennedy, Theresa Brophy, Helen Kiely

Emer McDonnell, Deirdre Hughes, Niamh Harkin.

Substitutes: Philomena Fogarty and Caitriona Hennessy replaced Helen Kiely and Niamh Harkin respectively.

Future prospects for Camogie look quite good, although at senior level the game will probably be dominated by less than ten counties for some time to come.

The junior All-Ireland competition was initiated in 1968 and to date 12 counties have claimed the title. An All-Ireland minor competition began in 1974 and a total of seven counties have captured that title since then.

In 1992, an All-Ireland intermediate grade was introduced and the honour of winning this crown has been well-spread. In the seven years of competition from 1992 to 1998, Clare took two titles while Donegal, Limerick, Tipperary, Down and Dublin took one each.

Between the four Camogie grades a total of fourteen counties have tasted All-Ireland success.

As with the games of hurling and football, the All-Ireland senior Camogie club championship has been a great success and has produced some stirring encounters. It began in 1964 and the title has been won by clubs from seven counties — Kilkenny (9), Wexford (6), Cork (5), Dublin (5), Galway (5), Limerick (4), and Tipperary (2).

The honour of the little village stirs all hearts.

GALWAY'S PLACE IN FOOTBALL GLORY

Galway is one of the leading 'dual' counties of Gaelic games — its teams excel at both hurling and football. Their All-Ireland title record (up to 2000), in all of the inter-county grades, is as follows:

	Football	Hurling
Senior	8	4
Junior	4	2
Under 21	1	7
Minor	5	4
Intermediate	no competition	1

In senior football Galway rank third in the honours list behind Dublin and the leaders, Kerry and it is the details of this achievement that this chapter records.

In 1900, Galway emerged, unopposed, as football champions of Connaught. That was followed by a walk-over from Antrim in the All-Ireland semi-final. It was poor preparation, however, for the Home Final against Tipperary who had had testing encounters with Cork, Limerick, Kerry and Kilkenny. (They lost to Kilkenny but succeeded with an objection, based on the fact that Kilkenny had the assistance of some Tipperary men on their team).

It was an era when the county champions represented the county in the All-Ireland campaign, but they did have the option of selecting players from other clubs within the county. In 1900, the Galway champions, Tuam Krugers, unwisely decided to go it alone and suffered a humiliating defeat from Tipperary on the score of 2:17 to 0:1.

Galway's next opportunity for All-Ireland honours came in 1919. This time they were better prepared. Roscommon fell to them in the Connaught final by 1:6 to 0:5. Galway then faced Kerry (who had notched up five All-Ireland crowns by then) in the All-Ireland semi-final. The game was a draw but Galway won the replay with two goals to spare — no fear of the Kingdom there. However, Galway's hour had not yet come. In the final they came up against a talented Kildare team captained by the great Larry Stanley. When the final whistle blew, Kildare were the victors on the score of 2:5 to 0:1.

In 1922, Galway reached the All-Ireland final of that year in rather unusual circumstances. They lost the Connaught final to Sligo by 1 point — the score: Sligo 3:2; Galway 1:7. Sligo then proceeded to defeat Tipperary in the All-Ireland semi-final and looked forward to a show-down with Dublin in the final. But it wasn't to be. A replay of the Connaught final was ordered and a Galway victory qualified them for a place in the All-Ireland final on 7 October 1922.

Dublin, backboned by the McDonnells, Johnny and Paddy; the Synotts, Joe and John and that great dual player, Kildare-born Frank Burke, were the outstanding football team of that time. They would be hard to beat; and so it was for Galway. In a low-scoring game — six points to four — with defences dominating, Galway had to be satisfied with second best, yet again.

When they took their first All-Ireland crown in 1925 it came from a bizarre set of circumstances, which were dealt with in detail in my book *Off the Field and On* (Wolfhound Press, 1999). In brief, this is what happened that year. Cavan and Kerry, champions of their respective provinces, were both suspended after their All-Ireland semi-final encounter. Mayo, who had been nominated by the Connaught council to represent the province, defeated the Leinster title-holders, Wexford, and having survived an objection were declared All-Ireland champions. But not for long. In a delayed Connaught final Galway defeated Mayo by 2 points and became the official title-holders.

Mick Donnellan was a member of that successful team. A generation later, his son, John, starred in the Galway successes of 1964,

1965 and 1966; he had the honour of captaining the team in 1964. The family link with Galway football success continued into a third generation when Michael, son of John and grandson of Mick, gave a capital display in the All-Ireland final of 1998 and was honoured with the Texaco Footballer of the Year Award.

In 1934, Galway avenged the 2-point defeat of 1922, at the hands of Dublin, in a spectacular game that ended on the score: Galway 3:5; Dublin 1:9 — a winning margin of 2 points in favour of Galway resulting in a second All-Ireland crown for the men from the west. Galway had some fine strong footballers, among them Mick Higgins, Dinny O'Sullivan, John Dunne, Mick Connaire, Martin Kelly and Brendan Nestor.

Four years later, in 1938, and back-boned by the stalwart players of 1934, Galway, after a Connaught victory over Mayo and a semi-final win over Monaghan, faced Kerry in the final at Croke Park, on 25 September. In terms of All-Ireland victories at that time, the scales tipped heavily in Kerry's favour at twelve titles to two. However, displaying scant regard for tradition and the honours list, Galway forced a draw in a game that provided a wonderful exhibition of Gaelic football. Thus the final went to a replay, on 23 October. Up to then, there had been four All-Ireland final replays in the history of the championship. Kerry had participated in the previous three and had been victorious on each occasion. It represented another plus on the Kerry side of the scales. However, Galway were unfazed. No doubt, they had in mind their 1919 All-Ireland semi-final replay victory over the men from the Kingdom.

The 1938 replay was a game of hard physical exchanges — not one for the purists. Galway led at half-time by 1:3 to 0:4. On resumption, Kerry added a point to cut the deficit. Galway's reply was swift. A well-taken free by John Burke landed in the Kerry square and ended up in the net. Indeed, so hectic and congested was the mêlée in the Kerry goal-mouth that the identity of the player who caused the ball to cross the goal-line was never established.

With two minutes to go, Galway led by 2:4 to 0:6. The referee blew for a Kerry free and, just as it was taken, he blew again for another Kerry free as a Galway player had been standing too close. The crowd, understandably, took it to be the final whistle and rushed onto the pitch to cheer their heroes. Confusion reigned for a long time but eventually the game was restarted and two more minutes were played. Kerry, with a much-changed line-out — many of their players had already departed from Croke Park — added a point from a free before the final whistle. Galway took their third All-Ireland crown amid scenes of wild jubilation.

Success over Kerry always added that extra glow to victory — a victory in this case that was fashioned from the opportunism of the Galway forwards, the place-kicking of midfielder John Burke, the display of a brilliant defence that was marshalled around Mick Connaire, at full back and Bobby Beggs, at centre back, both of whom were brilliant in their respective positions.

Lean years followed for Galway before a golden era dawned for them. During the years 1956 to 1966, inclusive, Galway contested every Connaught football final, winning nine of them. Only in 1961 and 1962 did they lose — to Roscommon — and on each occasion by just 1 point. They went on to contest six All-Ireland finals and won four of them. The first victory came in 1956 over a Cork team that had left their shooting boots at home.

I watched Galway lose to Kerry in 1959; I thought the final score, of 3:7 to 1:4, rather flattered the Kerrymen. Kerry were captained that day by that supreme footballing perfectionist, Mick O'Connell. It was an era when Mick, a native of Valentia Island, had to travel by boat to the mainland.

Star of the day was Kerry's right half-back Sean Murphy from Camp, who received the Texaco Footballer of the Year Award. However, for me, the key to Kerry's victory lay in the manner in which Niall Sheehy, at full back, and Kevin Coffey, at centre half-back, coped with the wiles and stratagems of 'the Terrible Twins', Sean Purcell and Frankie Stockwell, who alternated from time to time throughout the game, but to no avail.

Greatness, and a place among the élite, came for Galway when they won three All-Ireland titles in a row from 1964 to 1966, inclusive. They joined a select band of counties that had captured three or more All-Ireland crowns in a row.

The list reads as follows:

Dublin   1897, 1898, 1899
          1906, 1907, 1908
          1921, 1922, 1923

Wexford 1915, 1916, 1917, 1918

Kerry   1929, 1930. 1931. 1932
         1939, 1940, 1941
         1978, 1979, 1980, 1981
         1984, 1985, 1986.

Galway   1964, 1965, 1966.

In 1964, the only survivor from the successful team of 1956 was
Mattie McDonagh — a midfielder in that year, but a brilliant centre
forward on the three-in-a-row teams. At the time of writing, he still
remains the only Connaught man to hold four All-Ireland Senior
football medals.

In all, twelve Galway players participated in all three of the
1964–1966 All-Ireland successes (as shown in the table on page 184).

In each of the years in question, it was a Galway player who
captured The Texaco Footballer of the Year Award:

1964 Full back, Noel Tierney
1965 Left half-back, Martin Newell
1966 Centre forward, Mattie McDonagh

Galway had a potent attack that combined expertly, moved well off
the ball, used the open spaces to telling effect, and spread-eagled many
a defence. Their own defence was rocklike — a great full back line in
Enda Colleran, Noel Tierney and John Bosco McDermott, and behind
them, Johnny Geraghty in goal. In the three finals, no goal was
conceded by Galway and, interestingly, they scored only one goal
themselves, in the 1966 game. The results of the three matches were as
follows:

1964 v Kerry 0:15 to 0:10

1965 v Kerry 0:12 to 0:9

1966 v Meath 1:10 to 0:7.

Galway made history in 1965. Not only was it the first time that Kerry lost two finals in a row, but it fell to Galway to deprive them of victory on both occasions.

The 1966 final was a game of tactics. Galway were meeting a strong, high-fielding Meath team. From the outset Galway played the ball low and to great effect. It left Meath somewhat bewildered and completely removed any superiority that they might have had in a high-fielding game.

Indeed, this Galway team almost made it four in a row. A 2-point win over Kerry, the reigning All-Ireland champions, in the All-Ireland semi-final of 1963 was a good indication of their class and quality. They looked set to take the title against Dublin until disaster struck. The defensive set-up that was to cover a sideline kick to Dublin, from near the 14-yard line on the Cusack Stand side near Hill 16, was found wanting. In the words of Des Ferguson, the Dublin full forward and hero of many an hour, '... two or three of our forwards were lined up to put the ball in the net.'

After the three-in-a-row triumph, All-Ireland success deserted Galway footballers. A long, lean spell followed for them. A whole generation grew up starved of success. As the 1990s drew to a close, few people in Galway under 40 years of age would have had any memories of 1966, and so, had no glorious memories to talk about and relive. However, all of that was to completely change. The season of 1998 brought new heroes, All-Ireland success and wonderful celebrations.

The Galway team improved as it progressed through the different stages of the championship that year. Fate and fortune favoured them in a Connaught final encounter against Roscommon that was only won after a draw, and a replay that went to extra time. In the All-Ireland semi-final against Derry, however, there was no disputing the better team.

Galway Team Members of the 1960s

Galway	1963 (lost) v Dublin	1964 v Kerry	1965 v Kerry	1966 v Meath
M. Moore	✓			
Enda Colleran	✓	✓	✓ (c)	✓ (c)
Noel Tierney	✓	✓	✓	✓
Sean Meade	✓	✓	✓	✓
John Bosco McDermott	✓	✓	✓	✓
John Donnellan	✓	✓ (c)	✓	✓ (sub)
Martin Newell	✓	✓	✓	✓
Mick Garrett	✓ (c)	✓	✓	
Mick Reynolds	✓	✓	✓ (sub)	
Cyril Dunne	✓	✓	✓	✓
Matty McDonagh	✓	✓	✓	✓
Pat Donnellan	✓		✓	✓
John Keenan	✓	✓	✓	✓
Sean Cleary	✓	✓	✓	✓
Seamus Leyden	✓	✓	✓	✓
B. Geraghty	✓ (sub)			
John Geraghty		✓	✓	✓
Christy Tyrrell		✓	✓	
Colie McDonagh				✓
Jimmy Duggan				✓
Liam Sammon				✓

Eleven Galwaymen played in four of the above finals
and twelve played in all three of the victories

Inspired by their trainer, John O'Mahony, Galway faced Kildare with confidence in the All-Ireland final. Kildare had been trained to the ounce by that great man from Kerry, Mick O'Dwyer, and were making their first All-Ireland final appearance since 1935 (when they lost to Cavan by four points).

Prior assessment and analysis led one to the conclusion that the game would be a 50–50 affair. Luck and tactics would decide the issue. And so it proved. Galway concentrated mainly on direct football — the old style of catch and kick. It conserved energy. It was a trump card. It led directly to a great goal shortly after the second half resumed.

John Devilly, playing fine football at centre half-back, sent a long clearance that was gathered by Michael Donnellan; his precision pass to Padraig Joyce was finished to the net. That, and an earlier point from Jarlath Fallon, represented the difference between the teams at the end of the match.

Captain and right half-back Ray Silke, proudly accepted the Sam Maguire Cup from fellow countyman, and President of the GAA, Joe McDonagh.

It was Galway's eighth All-Ireland victory and Sam was on its way to the City of the Tribes for the seventh time.

The Victorious Galway Team of 1998

The heroes of 1998 lined out as follows

Martin McNamara

Tomás Meehan, Gary Fahy, Tomás Mannion

Ray Silke (Captain), John Devilly, Seán De Paor

Kevin Walsh, Seán Ó Domhnaill

Michael Donnellan, Jarlath Fallon, Shay Walsh

Derek Savage, Padraig Joyce, Niall Finnegan.

Paul Clancy replaced Shay Walsh during the game.

THE ARTANE BOYS BAND

The Artane Boys Band was founded by the Irish Christian Brothers in 1872. It was to become the most famous band in Ireland and gave its first GAA performance on 14 June 1886.

The band's name has become synonymous with Croke Park on All-Ireland final day — a tradition that dates from 1889. It has led the giants and the legends of the GAA world around Croke Park and we have become so accustomed to this group of musicians that we take their presence almost for granted. However, this does not mean that the band is not appreciated. With its members always immaculately dressed in their blue and scarlet outfits, the band brings a special glamour to Croke Park on final day. This unique group entertains the crowd with its musicianship, figure-marching and a splendid variety of tunes, ranging from stirring ballads to county 'specials'.

The founder of the Artane Boys Band was Thomas Alphonsus Hoope, the first Superior of Artane — a visionary with an eye for talent. He spared no effort in ensuring that any one with ability developed it to its full potential. He was born of Quaker parents at Richill, County Armagh in 1817 and died in 1899 leaving us a wonderful musical legacy.

The Industrial School in Artane was run by the Christian Brothers to educate underprivileged boys. It was closed in 1969 and until then, membership of the band was confined only to its pupils. After that members were recruited from other schools in Dublin.

Gaelic fans, understandably, associate the band primarily with Croke Park on All-Ireland final day. However, that is only a small part of the band's programme. Not everyone is aware that it has fulfilled engagements in every county in Ireland and that it has also performed overseas. The band's first foreign trip was in 1884 when it performed in London. The next visit abroad wasn't until 1958 when it went to Wembley to play at the Gaelic games during the Whit week-end. It also performed on BBC Television for 'In Town Tonight' during this visit.

The band's first performance in the US was in 1962; it was to be the first of many there. It will come as no surprise to learn that in the early tours of America, the Artane Boys Band entertained and delighted packed houses in Boston, Cleveland, Detroit, New York, Philadelphia and Pittsburgh.

In the 1980s, it led the St Patrick's Day Parade in Toronto on one occasion, and also performed at the world-famous Skydome.

A foreign musician critic wrote of the Artane Boys Band: 'I have heard and enjoyed many bands in many countries but I can recall none to surpass the Artane Boys. The extent of their repertoire simply amazed me'. Little wonder, for as well as Irish tunes, stirring ballads and county 'specials', the band has endeared itself to audiences with recitals from the works of Bach, Von Suppe, Verdi, Sibelius, Wagner, Romberg, Sousa and many other great composers.

When Bing Crosby visited Ireland in September 1961, the band played for him at Dublin Airport and he commented: 'I've never heard any band composed of youthful musicians play with such tone and expression'. Other famous personalities who were honoured to have heard the Artane Boys Band include Cardinal Cushing, President John F. Kennedy and Princess Grace of Monaco.

So as to ensure the long-term future of the band, a fund-raising campaign was undertaken in 1992 with a target of £400,000. The campaign was spearheaded by a group of outstanding GAA personalities under the following structure:

Patrons
Dr Patrick Hillery, former President of Ireland,
Micheál O'Hehir

Trustees

John Heneghen CFC
Jack Lynch
Peadar Ó Cuinn

Fund Executives

Paddy Buggy, Paddy McFlynn, Séamus Ó Riain
John Dowling, Padraig Ó Fainín, Seán Ó Síocháin,
Dr Mick Loftus, Conchúr Ó Murchú
(Seven former Presidents of the GAA and a retired Director
General.)

Development Committee

P.P. Guthrie (Chairman), Nicky English, Frank O'Rourke,
Matt Browne, John O'Connell, Jack O'Shea,
Sean Condon, Liam O'Maolmhichíl, Pat Quigley,
Paddy Cullen, Micheál Ó Muircheartaigh.

The campaign had three main objectives:-
- To purchase new instruments as the band had been using the same ones since the late 1960s.
- To purchase new uniforms. The existing ones dated from the early 1970s and were made from material brought by Micheál O'Hehir from the United States of America.
- To renovate the Bandroom Complex. Very little had been done in this area for over a century.

The GAA demonstrated its appreciation of, and commitment to, the Artane Boys Band by contributing £115,000 to the campaign.
Funds were also raised through:

- Four Provincial Golf Classics
- The Friends of the Artane Boys Band
- The Corporate Sector.

Membership of the band is open to boys from the age of nine years and upwards; they must retire from the band at the age of sixteen. No wonder the band, sometimes referred to as 'The Biggest Little Band in the World', never grows old. The performing band consists of about seventy-five boys and the average age is just under fourteen years.

Membership of the band provides many opportunities for character building, leadership and personality development. The youngest members attend the Band Complex each afternoon from Monday to Friday and receive one hour's tuition in theory and music each day. The senior members also attend from Monday to Friday, for two-hour rehearsal sessions. In all, a total of 250 boys attend rehearsal and tuition sessions each week.

Many past pupils make their living as musicians and are to be found in organisations such as Symphony and Light Orchestras, Army and Police Bands, Dance Bands and the Army School of Music.

In 1988, the Artane Senior Band was formed. This initiative came from past members and its membership is drawn from graduates of the boys' band.

All those involved in The Artane Boys Band Development Fund deserve our deepest thanks and appreciation. They have ensured the future of a great National asset that has contributed so much to preserving and promoting distinctive aspects of our cultural identity.

MEDIA COVERAGE

In the early days of the Association, coverage of Gaelic Games by the national press was sparse and indeed, at times, non-existent. As a consequence, one sometimes finds conflicting details of score lines and team line-outs when perusing records from those days. Even as late as 1939, after the Cork v Kilkenny All-Ireland hurling final, a Monday morning newspaper carried the headline, 'Leahy's last minute point secures the honours', when in fact, it was Jimmy Kelly who scored the historic winner.

Gradually, however, this all changed. Previews and reviews in the national daily newspapers grew in importance and content. Analysis and detail were presented in greater depth and journalists began to visit training grounds where they interviewed mentors and players. Public interest grew and grew as the published articles whetted peoples' appetites.

Down through the decades, the world of journalism produced many brilliant writers who devoted their talents to the cause and development of Gaelic games. They were idealists, imbued with a fervent national spirit.

Thomas F. O'Sullivan, author of *The Story of the GAA*, which was published in 1916 and covered the period 1884–1908; Phil O'Neill ('Sliabh Ruadh'), author of *History of the GAA 1910–1930* (Kilkenny Journal Ltd, circa 1932); his friend Seamus Upton ('Vigilant'); Paddy D. Mehigan, ('Carbery'), whose yearly publication *Carbery's Annual*, was highly sought after; Pádraig Puirséal, whose lifelong dedication to our games, gave us *The GAA in its Time* (The Purcell Family, 1982); the productions of Séamus Ó Ceallaigh, in conjunction with Sean Murphy — all of these writers have left us with invaluable material.

There were also the newspaper journalists of my youth who produced wonderful articles: 'Fear Ciúin', 'Green Flag', John D. Hickey, Mick Dunne, Paddy Downey and Joe Sherwood; many people used to buy the *Evening Press* primarily to read Joe's articles entitled 'In the Soup'.

In more recent times, we have had brilliant analytical contributions from many journalists including Con Houlihan, Tom Humphries, Kevin Cashman, Denis Walsh and Enda McEvoy. Words are their stock in trade. They use them with all the skill and imagination of an architect as they build pictures and the minds of their readers develop and interpret the images.

To the *Irish Press*, now sadly defunct, must go much of the credit for initiating a wider coverage of GAA affairs and its games. From the founding of this newspaper, in 1931, it devoted much space to Gaelic games, with Joe Sherwood playing a leading journalistic rôle. *The Evening Press* was the first paper to give decent coverage to camogie and ladies' football and its competitors were then forced to follow suit.

In 1926, 2RN, subsequently known as Radio Éireann, was established. (I am told that the first voice to be heard from that station was that of Douglas Hyde.)

Thomas F. O'Sullivan

The speed at which the opportunity was seized to broadcast a Gaelic match was quite remarkable. P.S. O'Hegarty was the prime mover in this regard; he was a Corkman, a great hurling enthusiast and Secretary of the Department of Posts and Telegraphs. Following discussions with Paddy Mehigan (Carbery) it was agreed that he (Carbery) would do a broadcast. Thus it came about that the first broadcast of a Gaelic match was from Croke Park, on 29 August 1926, when Kilkenny and Galway met in the All-Ireland hurling semi-final of that year.

The following month, on 12 September 1926, the Munster final took place, in Cork, between Cork and Tipperary. 'Carbery' did a broadcast from the sideline but after twenty minutes the game had to be abandoned when an overcapacity crowd encroached onto the pitch. There were those who feared that such broadcasting would affect attendances. However, wiser heads, including the GAA President of the day, William P. Clifford of Limerick, thought otherwise — and they were right. Broadcasting proved to be a great advertisement for Gaelic games and the crowds at matches grew even bigger.

Phil O'Neill, 'Sliabh Ruadh'

Those broadcasts of 1926 Gaelic Games are believed to be the first field games broadcast live anywhere in the world.

A year later, in England, the FA Cup final between Arsenal and Cardiff was broadcast by the BBC. Before the match the vast assembly sang 'Abide with Me'. Cardiff won 1:0 — the first and only time to date that a non-English club has won the Cup.

I find it strange that Phil O'Neill (Sliabh Ruadh), in his excellent *History of the GAA from 1910–1930* (Kilkenny Journal Ltd, circa 1932), made no reference at all to the broadcasts. In his introduction he wrote: 'Níl anseo ach cúntas geárr ar ghach rud tabhachtach do thuit amach ó bhlian 1910 go 1930'. Perhaps he didn't approve, or maybe he felt live broadcasting of the games had no future.

Micheál O'Hehir arrived on the scene in 1938. I can remember his broadcasts from the mid-1940s onwards. Unlike today, you had to wait until late on Sunday night to get all the GAA match results from Seán Ó Ceallacháin. The National League hurling final of 1947, between Limerick and Kilkenny, took place in November of that year. Only a portion of the match was broadcast and I can remember as we sat at the table at teatime — I think it was after the news — Micheál O'Hehir came on air and announced that: 'the game ended in a thrilling and exciting draw, Limerick 4:5; Kilkenny 2:11'.

Earlier that year, Micheál had broadcast
the All-Ireland football final from the Polo
Grounds, New York. It was a milestone in
sports broadcasting.

In 1949, Micheál Ó Muircheartaigh
arrived on the scene. I believe it is true to
say that we were then blessed with two of
the best radio sports broadcasters that the
world has known. Their broadcasts played
a major rôle in popularising and promoting
Gaelic games and each broadcast provided
the raw material for discussion, dialogue
and debate among Gaelic followers.

Then came television. Again, fears that
new broadcasting technology would cause
a drop in attendances were unfounded.
Indeed, the opposite happened. It may
surprise many to learn that the first GAA
match to be televised live was a hurling   *Paddy Mehigan, 'Carbery'*
match at Gaelic Park, New York in 1951.

In Ireland, the first GAA matches to be televised live were the
Railway Cup finals on St Patrick's Day, 1962. Leinster defeated Munster
(in hurling) and Ulster (in football) to complete a double that year. It
was a very special day for Dublin's outstanding dual player, the late Des
Foley, who played centre-field for Leinster in both games.

The All-Ireland finals of 1962 — Tipperary v Wexford in hurling
and Kerry v Roscommon in football — were the first championship
finals to be televised. The commentary arrangement, however, was
rather unusual. It was decided that Seán Óg Ó Ceallacháin would do
the first quarter in English followed by Micheál Ó Muirceartaigh for
the next quarter, in Irish. It didn't appeal to the public and was
discontinued.

The TV picture in those days was, of course, black and white and
unless one of the teams wore white togs and the other a different
colour, distinguishing between them wasn't always easy. It also helped if
one of the teams wore a hooped jersey and the other wore a patterned

one. While football came across quite well, the speed of hurling presented problems which were only resolved as technology developed and improved.

In 1971, we saw our first All-Ireland final in colour when the blue and gold of Tipperary and the black and amber of Kilkenny appeared on the television screens. Victory went to Tipperary with a score of 5:17 to 5:14 on that occasion.

Since those days, disappointed ticket-seekers have had a very good second-best by virtue of being able to watch major games on television. Indeed, all they miss is the atmosphere of the occasion and the panoramic view of the entire pitch. On the other hand, they see far more detail and close-up activity on the screen.

Thanks to the media, we have benefited greatly with our national games, over the years, through three stages of communication. Reading has been provided by the journalists, listening by the radio commentators and viewing by the technology of television.

Nowadays, all three are available and, together, they provide us with wonderful recreation and entertainment.

Nostalgia

In 1980, the GAA decided to honour a great football and hurling personality from the past at the All-Star Reception which was to be held every year. On these occasions it was always very moving to witness the giants from the past — now venerable in appearance — receive their trophy of recognition. For them, the event conjured up nostalgic moments. To be close to these heroes of times past at these ceremonies, as I was on two occasions, revealed how much it means to them to be remembered.

The following is a brief pen picture of those who have been honoured — great men all:

The Footballers

Larry Stanley, Kildare (1980)

Larry was a wonderful athlete, a high-jump champion and a competitor at the 1924 Paris Olympic Games. He captained Kildare to All-Ireland victory over Galway in 1919 and won his second All-Ireland medal with Dublin in 1923. Those were the days before the Declaration Rule came into being and you could play only for the county in which you resided. In 1926, he was back with Kildare but they lost to Kerry in a replay by one goal in a football final classic. Larry, a brilliant midfielder, was a gentleman both on and off the field.

Tommy Murphy, Laois (1981)

Tommy was known as 'The Boy Wonder' as he had made his senior début at sixteen years of age. He was from Graiguecullen and was a delightful footballer who starred with his native Laois and also with Leinster in the 1930s and 1940s. He won Leinster titles as well as Railway Cup honours. In 1984, the centenary year of the GAA, a special panel made a selection of two centenary teams — one made up of players who had won All-Ireland medals, and the other from players who hadn't; Tommy was honoured by being chosen for the latter.

Paddy Moclair, Mayo (1982)

Paddy was a member of a fine Mayo team that won All-Ireland honours in 1936 following victories over Galway, after a replay in Connaught; Kerry, at the semi-final stage; and Laois, in the final. Paddy was a forward and played inter-provincial football for Connaught for many years. He won Railway Cup medals in 1934, 1936, 1937 and 1938.

Jim McCullagh, Armagh (1983)

Jim was one of Gaelic football's great defenders. He was an outstanding centre back and equally effective in the full-back line. His prowess on the football field was seen to full advantage when he played with Ulster in the Railway Cup competition. He tasted defeat in the finals of 1936, 1939 and 1941. However, reward came in 1942 with a sweet five-point victory over a Munster team (star-studded with fourteen Kerrymen as well as Eamon Young of Cork). Ulster retained the crown the following year with a one-point win over Leinster but lost it again in 1944. Jim was still playing in defence with Ulster, in 1947, when they took a six-point win over Leinster. This victory earned him a third and well-deserved Railway Cup medal — just rewards for many years of sterling service.

John Dunne, Galway (1984)

John was both player and mentor. He lined-out in Croke Park on All-Ireland final day on five occasions. A fearless midfielder, he tasted victory in 1934 with a two-point win over Dublin and again in 1938 with a great win over mighty Kerry, after a replay. He experienced defeat in 1933, 1940 and 1941 when Galway had to give way, only

narrowly, to Cavan (1933) and Kerry (1940 and 1941). He achieved
Railway Cup honours in 1934, 1937 and 1938.

J.J. Landers (Purty) and Tim Landers (Roundy), Kerry (1985)

In the annals of football, Landers (from Tralee) is a famous family
name. There were three brothers: Bill, Tim and John Joe — all quality
forwards. Bill won an All-Ireland medal in 1924, when Kerry beat
Dublin, on the score 4 points to 3. He came on as a substitute in 1932
when Kerry defeated Mayo in the All-Ireland final of that year.

John Joe was part of Kerry's great four-in-a-row success which ran
from 1929 to 1932 inclusive. He won his fifth All-Ireland medal in
1937.

Tim's All-Ireland successes began in 1931 and 1932 and two more
titles came his way in 1937 and 1939. He won his fifth All-Ireland
medal when he came on as a sub against Galway in 1941.

All three brothers took part in Kerry's All-Ireland victory of 1932.

Alf Murray, Armagh (1986)

Alf played for many years with Armagh and Ulster and manned the
centre forward position with distinction. He won Railway Cup medals
in 1942 and 1943 in the company of fellow countymen Jim McCullagh
and E. McLoughlin. He was honoured by being made the President of
the GAA in 1964.

Mick Higgins, Cavan (1987)

Mick was born in New York, in 1922, and returned to that city, in 1947,
to play the All-Ireland final against Kerry, at the Polo Grounds. He was
a brilliant centre forward and won three All-Ireland medals — the first
two in 1947 and 1948, and his third in 1952 when he captained the
Cavan team. He was a regular on the Ulster Railway Cup team and won
medals in 1947 and 1950 — again operating in the centre forward
position. In a long career, he won a total of seven Ulster title medals.

Kevin Armstrong, Antrim (1988)

Kevin was one of Gaelic games' great dual performers, who played
hurling and football for both Antrim and Ulster. In 1984, he was
chosen at left half-forward on the centenary team of hurlers who had

never won an All-Ireland medal. He was a member of the now defunct O'Connell's Club, in Belfast, and won four Railway Cup medals in all. He became the first man to take the Railway Cup trophy across the border when he captained Ulster to victory in 1947.

Peter McDermott, Meath (1989)

This genial and modest sportsman from the Royal county was known to all followers of Gaelic games as 'the man with the cap'. He was a potent left corner forward on both the Meath and Leinster teams. He won All-Ireland honours in 1949 and 1954 when Meath took victories over counties Cavan and Kerry, respectively. He also won a total of five Leinster titles. His only Railway Cup victory came very early on in his career; that was in 1944 when he played at left half-forward for Leinster who defeated Ulster in the final. During the period from 1940 to 1954, he won six Leinster medals and two National League medals. He also had the distinction of refereeing the All-Ireland finals of 1953 and 1956.

Eddie Boyle, Louth (1990)

Eddie was one of Louth's greatest footballers, and ranks among the best full backs the game has known. He was selected in 1984 at full back on the centenary team of players who had never won an All-Ireland medal. He was brilliant in Louth's Leinster campaign of 1943 when they bridged a thirty-one-year gap by defeating Laois in the Leinster final. They failed to a great Roscommon team in the All-Ireland semi-final. Eddie was a regular on Leinster Railway Cup teams for over twelve years and he became the only Louth man to win five Railway Cup medals.

Sean Purcell, Galway (1991)

Sean was a brilliant and highly versatile footballer. He won his first Railway Cup medal in 1951 when he partnered Gerry O'Malley of Roscommon at midfield for Connaught. Operating at centre forward he won further Railway Cup medals in 1957 and 1958. By the late 1950s, he had established a great partnership understanding with full forward Frankie Stockwell which led to them being dubbed 'The Terrible Twins'. When playing with Galway they would, on occasion, alternate their key forward positions with a view to unsteadying the opposing defence. Sean won his only All-Ireland medal, in 1956, when Galway were victorious over Cork. He was selected at centre forward on the centenary team of 1984.

Sean Flanagan, Mayo (1992)

Sean had been a pupil at St Jarlath's College, Tuam and had a determined and steely personality. He played at left full back when he captained Mayo to All-Ireland wins in 1950 and 1951. He was selected in the same position on the centenary Team in 1984. Sean was one of a small band of captains to have collected the Sam Maguire Cup on two occasions. In a career which lasted for fourteen years he also won two National League medals together with one Railway Cup medal, in the 1951 competition, when he captained Connaught.

Jimmy Murray, Roscommon (1993)

Jimmy, that great son of Knockcroghery and brilliant centre forward, led Roscommon to All-Ireland victory twice — in 1943, after a replay with Cavan, and in 1944 against Kerry. Jimmy's brother, Phelim, was also a member of the great Roscommon team of that era. A regular with Connaught, Jimmy was unlucky in that no Railway Cup was won by the western province during his time. He belongs to an élite band of players who captained his county to All-Ireland honours on two occasions.

Bill Delaney, Laois (1994)

Bill was a member of a great footballing clan from Stradbally, County Laois. There were six Delaneys, (including Bill) on the Laois team of 1936 that lost to Mayo in the All-Ireland final. For over a dozen years, throughout the 1930s and 1940s, he performed at top level for Laois and Leinster. He was masterly as both a midfielder and a centre forward. His achievements included four Leinster title medals and five Railway Cup victories. Among the highlights of a great career was the trip to America with the Laois football team on the *SS Manhattan*, in 1938.

The following is my own line-out of these great footballing stars in team format:

Paddy Moclair (Mayo)

Eddie Boyle (Louth)

John Dunne (Galway)   Sean Flanagan (Mayo)

Jim McCullagh (Armagh)

John Joe Landers (Kerry)   Tim Landers (Kerry)

Larry Stanley (Kildare), Tommy Murphy (Laois)

Mick Higgins (Cavan)
or
Bill Delaney(Laois)

Alf Murray (Armagh)   Jimmy Murray (Roscommon)

Sean Purcell (Galway)

Kevin Armstrong (Antrim),   Peter McDermott (Meath)

As there was no goalkeeper among All-Star Reception Award winners to choose from, I had to find someone to man the gap. I picked Paddy Moclair — he would have played anywhere and done a good job. With too many forwards I had to take a little poetic licence and play the Landers brothers in the half-back line: they would perform well in any position.

J. McCullagh   T. Landers   J.J. Landers   B. Landers   E. Boyle   S. Purcell

S. Flanagan   P. McDermott   T. Murphy   P. Moclair   B. Delaney   K. Armstrong

The Hurlers

Mick Mackey, Limerick (1980)

'Munster's pride and Limerick's glory' — Mick could play in any position on the field for he had all the necessary qualities. However, the name Mick Mackey is synonymous with the centre forward position. He was probably the greatest exponent of centre-forward play that the game of hurling has ever known. The crowd loved him and he loved the glory and the drama, and every challenge of the hurling arena. His county career stretched from 1930–1947. He was selected at the centre forward position on the centenary team of All-Ireland medal winners, in 1984.

Jack Lynch, Cork (1981)

Where we sported and played 'neath each green leafy glade
On the banks of my own lovely Lee ...

On social occasions Jack would often sing a few bars of 'The Banks'. This great dual player scaled the heights in both hurling and football. However, hurling was his forte and his first love. He became Taoiseach of his country, but never lost the common touch. Jack was arguably the most popular Irish politician of this century: when he stood down as Taoiseach, Liam Cosgrave said, '... Jack Lynch was the most popular politician in the country since O'Connell.' He won six All-Ireland senior medals in a row, from 1941 to 1946 inclusive (1945 in football), and this record looks likely to stand for ever and a day. Jack played at the top level of Gaelic games from 1935 to 1951. He was selected at centrefield on the centenary team of All-Ireland medal winners, in 1984.

Garret Howard, Limerick (1982)

Garret was the only Limerick man to win five All-Ireland senior hurling medals — two with Dublin and three with his native county, Limerick. He also hurled with Tipperary in the early 1930s. He formed part of a powerful half-back line for the four years from 1933 to 1936, inclusive, when he won four Munster title medals and two All-Ireland medals. This line-out was: Mickey Cross, Paddy Clohessy, Garret Howard.

He was a great enthusiast who loved all sports; his hurling career, at county level, ended in 1936 after a 15-year innings.

Pa 'Fowler' McInerney, Clare (1983)

Pa won his first All-Ireland medal in 1914 when he played in goal with Clare. He won his second, and last, in 1927 with his adopted county, Dublin, playing at full back. He must have been the oldest ever full back to play in an All-Ireland final as he was 39 years of age when Clare played Kilkenny in 1932. He played at top level for almost 20 years. How he would have loved to have seen Clare's performances during the 1990s.

Jimmy Langton, Kilkenny (1984)

Jimmy was one of Kilkenny's great hurling stylists and ranks among the greatest half-forwards that the game has known. He was on the Kilkenny team on two occasions when they won the All-Ireland title — both memorable victories. The first of these was in the midst of thunder and lightning and rain — in 1939 when Kilkenny pipped Cork by a last-minute point from the stick of Jimmy Kelly. The weather was kinder on the second occasion, in 1947, when Cork fell again to Kilkenny in a classic final. Once more the margin of victory was also only one point — and again it was scored in the dying moments of the game, compliments of Terry Leahy. Jimmy was selected at left half-forward on the GAA's centenary team in 1984.

Eudi Coughlan, Cork (1985)

Eudi was the son of Patrick Coughlan (known as 'Parson') and nephew of Dan, Denis, Ger and Tom, all of whom had hurled and won All-Ireland medals with Cork. Hurling flowed freely in Eudi's blood. Blackrock and Cork are proud of this outstanding half-forward who played at all times with verve, enthusiasm and élan and adorned the game with sparkling manly performances. His twelve-year career, at the top level of the sport, ended in 1931.

Tommy Doyle, Tipperary (1986)

Between the years of 1937 and 1953 this accomplished hurler gave many sterling performances, playing in positions of both defence and

attack for Tipperary. Tommy's performances in opposition to Christy
Ring added to his immortality as a top hurler. Always superbly fit, he
was no mean footballer — or boxer either — and he could also sing a
good song.

Christy Moylan, Waterford (1987)

A Waterford dual performer and proud son of the Decies, he excelled
at left half-forward, where he turned in many stylish performances for
his county. Christy was also a very versatile player and could operate
effectively in many positions. Emigration, in search of work,
punctuated Christy's hurling career which lasted from 1935 to 1949
overall.

Paddy 'Fox' Collins, Cork (1988)

Paddy was a true blue at club and county level — dedicated, loyal and
committed — whether as player, administrator or selector. To him,
every task was important and no task was too great. Self-effacing and
modest he adorned the scene at club and county level with his
presence. He was left full back, for Cork, in the three epic games it took
to decide the All-Ireland final of 1931 against Kilkenny.

M.J. 'Inky' Flaherty, Galway (1989)

'Hurrah for the men of the West'. For decades Galwaymen kept the
hurling flag flying in Connaught. Through the 1940s and into the 1950s
'Inky' was one of those stalwart men who gave so much to the game.
The highlight of his career was in the Railway Cup victory of 1947. On
this occasion, the (all Galway) Connaught team took their first-ever
Railway Cup title when they beat a Munster side whose line-out reads
like a profile of hurling giants.

John Joe Doyle, Clare (1990)

At the time of writing (2000), this genial survivor of the 1932 All-
Ireland final was 94 years of age. He ranks among the top corner backs
that the game has ever known. Clean play and good sportsmanship
were his stock-in-trade in a career lasting from 1926 to 1938. He was in
Croke Park, in September 1995, to celebrate Clare's historic All-Ireland
win over Offaly.

Jackie Power, Limerick (1991)

Jackie is one of the immortals of the game. No greater, more versatile hurler has graced the green sward of any hurling arena; he could play in any position with remarkable effectiveness. He belonged to the Mackey era and his career lasted from 1935 to 1949.

Jackie was also an accomplished footballer. He passed on his prowess in this field to his son Ger who won eight All-Ireland football titles with Kerry.

Bobby Rackard and Billy Rackard, Wexford (1992)

Rackard is a name that proudly takes its place among the élite of hurling family names. There were four hurling sons who shared that surname: Nicky, Bobby, Billy and Jimmy. All of them played at some stage of the 1951 campaign with the Wexford team.

Bobby and Billy were brilliant defenders, ranking with the greatest the game has produced. Billy's career was the longer of the two, Bobby's having been cut short by a farming injury, in 1957, when he was 30 years of age. Billy found his niche in hurling when he settled into the rôle of centre back and he gave many majestic performances playing at that position. Bobby's display at full back, when he switched to that position in the second half of the 1954 All-Ireland final, will always be talked about. It was a display as close to perfection as you could ever wish to find.

Pat Stakelum, Tipperary (1993)

Pat gave many invincible displays at centre back which have placed him among the masters in that key rôle on the hurling field. He came to the fore in the glory days of Tipperary's three-in-a-row victories from 1949 to 1951, inclusive. One of his displays in that era saw him compared to Paddy Clohessy of Limerick and Jim Regan of Cork — you can't get better than that.

Martin White, Kilkenny (1994)

Martin was 91 years of age at the time of writing (2000). He is the only survivor from the Cork and Kilkenny teams that contested the 1931 All-Ireland final. He played in the first game of this battle, in which his opposite number was Jim Regan. He retired in 1938 having played in several forward positions for Kilkenny and in six All-Ireland finals, from which he brought home three winner's medals.

As with the footballers, I have made my own selection and lined-out these descendants of Cú Chulainn in team format:

Pa 'Fowler' McInerney (Clare)

Bobby Rackard (Wexford)

John Joe Doyle (Clare)   Paddy 'Fox' Collins (Cork)

Billy Rackard (Wexford)

Pat Stakelum (Tipperary)   Garret Howard (Limerick)

Jack Lynch (Cork) Christy Moylan (Waterford)

Jim Langton(Kilkenny) Mick Mackey (Limerick) Eudi Coughlan (Cork)

Jackie Power (Limerick)

M.J. 'Inky' Flaherty (Galway),   Tommy Doyle (Tipperary)
or
Martin White(Kilkenny).

Some team indeed — you could possibly pick as good but you won't pick better.

Sadly, since 1994, the annual practice of honouring a great hurling and football personality from the past has been discontinued.

One hopes that we will see the day when it will be revived again. It is important that a scheme should exist to honour the men from days gone by who brought so much entertainment to so many. It is a fitting tribute and for them the moment is very special.

P. McInerney   G. Howard   E. Coughlan   J.J. Doyle   T. Doyle

R. Rackard   W. Rackard   M.J. Flaherty   J. Power